RAINER TWIFORD and PETER CARSON have published papers and delivered presentations at professional meetings on various topics in psychology. Both are licensed practicing psychologists and have extensive experience working with children, adolescents, and their families. In addition, they have served as consultants to various social service agencies, schools, and courts involved with adolescents. Dr. Twiford is the author of *A Child with a Problem: A Guide to the Psychological Disorders of Children*, also published by Spectrum Books.

Rainer Twiford and Peter Carson

THE ADOLESCENT PASSAGE

TRANSITIONS FROM CHILD TO ADULT

A SPECTRUM BOOK

Prentice-Hall, Inc., Englewood Cliffs, New Jersey 07632

Library of Congress Cataloging in Publication Data

TWIFORD, RAINER, (date)
The adolescent passage.

(A Spectrum Book)
Bibliography: p.
Includes index.
1. Adolescence. 2. Adolescent psychology.
3. Parent and child. I. Carson, Peter, (date)
II. Title.
HQ796.T84   305.2'3   80-18641
ISBN 0-13-008714-9
ISBN 0-13-008706-8 (pbk)

*To our wives, Marsha and Joan
and our daughters, Eleanor and Elizabeth*

Editorial/production supervision and interior design by Carol Smith
Cover design by Peter Ross
Manufacturing buyer: Cathie Lenard

© 1980 by Prentice-Hall, Inc., *Englewood Cliffs, New Jersey 07632*

A SPECTRUM BOOK

10   9   8   7   6   5   4   3   2

Printed in the United States of America

PRENTICE-HALL INTERNATIONAL, INC., London
PRENTICE-HALL OF AUSTRALIA PTY. LIMITED, Sydney
PRENTICE-HALL OF CANADA, LTD., Toronto
PRENTICE-HALL OF INDIA PRIVATE LIMITED, New Delhi
PRENTICE-HALL OF JAPAN, INC., Tokyo
PRENTICE-HALL OF SOUTHEAST ASIA PTE. LTD., Singapore
WHITEHALL BOOKS LIMITED, Wellington, New Zealand

Contents

v

65539

Preface

As practicing psychologists, we have come to recognize that
adolescence is a unique period of human development.
There is a vast amount of material written about adolescence, yet the behavior of adolescents has too often been
ignored as a subject of scientific inquiry. We have combined
research findings with our clinical observations in order to
promote the reader's understanding of adolescence.

Some adults are frustrated in their attempts to understand much of the behavior of adolescents. Why do many
young people suddenly attach considerable importance to
the attitudes of their peers? What effect does rapid physical
growth have on the adolescent? Why is suicide a leading
cause of teenage deaths? Answers to these questions require
a fundamental understanding of the unique forces that de-

termine adolescent behavior. Lack of understanding of these variables may lead to ineptitude in dealing with teenagers. Also, the uninformed adult is vulnerable to experiencing such negative feelings as frustration, anger, hopelessness, despair, confusion, and helplessness. These emotions may further impede effective communication with the young person.

Our primary purpose in writing this book is threefold. First, we expose the reader to the critical factors that influence and shape the life of the adolescent. Second, we attempt to educate adults regarding the nature and treatment of several problems common to adolescence. Third, we offer practical methods for parents to use to improve relations with their teenagers.

We believe that a more enlightened approach to adolescence will enable adults who work and live with young people to develop more meaningful, fulfilling, and productive relationships with them. We hope to demonstrate that much of the anguish and frustration often associated with adolescence is unnecessary and can be avoided.

Acknowledgments

There are many people who aided in the preparation of this manuscript. We are extremely grateful to David Lail for his creative editorial contribution. Thanks are extended to the Clarksdale Public Library for its cooperation in acquiring helpful resource materials. Appreciation is also expressed

to Newton Dodson, Director of the Region I Mental Health
Center, for his encouragement and support. We also thank
Ann Bolm for her superior clerical and editorial assistance.
Finally, we acknowledge our families, to whom this book is
dedicated, for their patience and love.

part *I*

NORMAL
DEVELOPMENT
OF THE
ADOLESCENT

In the first section of this book we attempt to orient the reader to the nature and course of normal adolescent growth. Adolescence, as a stage of development, is defined. The most important and well-known theories of adolescence are discussed. The impact of physical and sexual development is explored here. Part I is designed to provide an overview of adolescence that will enable the reader to approach more specialized areas of this book with greater understanding.

chapter 1

What Is Adolescence?

Adolescence is the period of human development when children grow into adults. This transitional period is marked by rapid physical and behavioral change. Adolescents are encouraged to develop patterns of responsibility, independence, morality, intelligence, emotional stability, and other characteristics associated with maturity. However, legal and social sanctions prevent the adolescent from enjoying many of the freedoms and privileges granted adults. Hence, this time of change is fraught with unique difficulties and frustrations that often produce tremendous stress for these young people, as well as for their peers, parents, teachers, and other associates. This book attempts to explain the interesting phenomenon of adolescence, the unique problems it engenders, and useful methods of coping with the difficulties of this developmental period.

The word *adolescence* is derived from the Latin word *adolescere*, which means "to grow to maturity." Adolescence is the period when young people undergo radical changes in physiology, attitudes, and social relationships. Adolescence has been defined in terms of age, physical development, behavior, legal status, and social relationships. It is difficult to pinpoint the beginning and the end of the adolescent period.

There are no commonly accepted guidelines that distinguish childhood, adolescence, and adulthood. For the purposes of this text, adolescence is considered to begin after puberty (sexual maturity) and to end in the early twenties. The adolescent is, therefore, capable of sexual reproduction but has not attained adult status. This definition is necessarily arbitrary and cannot be applied in every case. For example, a nineteen-year-old person who is married and economically independent is, by most standards, considered an adult. On the other hand, the twenty-two-year-old person who is living in his or her parents' home and attending graduate school at their expense meets most of the criteria of adolescence. Even so, defining adolescence in the sense given earlier in this paragraph allows a flexibility commensurate with the numerous behavioral and social variables that shape this period of life.

ADOLESCENCE AS A PHENOMENON OF THE INDUSTRIAL AGE

One of the most interesting aspects of adolescence is that this period of adjustment is limited to industrially advanced cultures. In her 1937 study of Samoan young people, Margaret Mead discovered an absence of an extended transitional period from childhood to adulthood. Thus, she did not observe the troubled behavior patterns that are typically exhibited by young people in more technologically advanced societies. Other scholars studying the cultures of primitive nations substantiated Dr. Mead's observations of Samoan youth. Subsequent to further systematic study of anthropologists, sociologists, psychologists, and other scientists, an explanation of this phenomenon became apparent: Successful adaptation in industrially advanced societies requires a repertoire of highly specialized, sophisticated patterns of behavior. These specialized skills are acquired over many years of educational and social preparation. Hence, young people are forced to delay marriage, economic independence, and autonomous life-styles. On the other hand, the Samoan male's capacity to work is largely a function of physical maturity. The male usually follows his father into work shortly after puberty. The Samoan female is generally married soon after her first menstrual period. Therefore, there is no prolonged economic or social dependence on the family, nor are there socially induced restraints on sexual activity. Hence, the transition from childhood to adulthood is relatively devoid of the turmoil observed in industrial nations.

ADOLESCENCE AS AN ADJUSTMENT PERIOD

Contrary to popular opinion, several studies indicate that adolescence is not particularly different from other periods of development. For example, these studies demonstrate

6

that most teenagers enjoy increasing independence and responsibility and satisfying social relations. An abundance of problems and adjustment difficulties was not observed.

On the other hand, in some ways adolescence is viewed as a difficult period of growth. As mentioned, the adolescent is expected to show evidence of maturity. Adults expect adolescents to demonstrate academically, socially, and legally responsible behavior. Young people are encouraged to form mature social relations while exercising sexual restraint. Society demands that adolescents understand and obey the law, but younger adolescents are not allowed to participate fully in determining legal codes.

These and other paradoxes, coupled with radical alteration in physiology and rapidly changing social roles, contribute to special problems characteristic of the adolescent period. The emotions of adolescents may be quite variable and extremely sensitive. This is sometimes referred to as *heightened emotionality*. Adolescent emotionality may be marked by low tolerance for frustration, behavioral tics, quarrelsomeness, or a finicky appetite. General restlessness and rebellion against adult authority are sometimes characteristic of adolescence.

As society's expectations of the maturing adolescent change, acceptable roles and behavior patterns are quickly altered. As adolescents shift from roles of dependence to independence, they begin to rely more on the peer group rather than the family to supply information about acceptable codes of behavior. This information is used to create a unique identity that differentiates adolescents from their parents. As young people explore various roles and life-styles, they become acutely aware of information offered by others concerning their behavior. Hence, individual at-

What Is Adolescence?

titudes and feelings about themselves are largely determined by messages from others. Adolescents are highly sensitive to praise and criticism offered by peers. This creates a higher degree of conformity to the peer group than is generally observed in children or adults. The importance of feedback from peers decreases, however, once the individual has attained a reasonably fixed self-concept and has established a stable set of emotional, social, and vocational roles.

The heightened degree of peer influence and rapidly changing roles and expectations contribute to the problems of adolescent rebelliousness, alcohol and drug abuse, delinquency, suicide, depression, and self-starvation (anorexia nervosa). The nature and treatment of these problems are discussed in Part II of this book.

Factors that critically affect the normal development of adolescents are examined in Part I. Significant variables that are discussed in detail include physical change, peer influence (socialization), and the development of self-concept and personal identity. This discussion is intended to provide insight into the period that will enhance the reader's understanding of specific adolescent problems and methods of coping with them. Approaches to facilitating personal growth during adolescence are the topic of Part III, and adolescence as a transitional period is the topic of Part IV.

chapter 2

Physical Growth
and Maturation

Adolescence encompasses a period of accelerated physical growth and physiological change that marks the transition from child to adult. It is a period when physical sexual maturity is reached and the ability to reproduce is attained. Only during the first two years of life is the rate of physical growth greater.

The physical changes that occur, especially during early adolescence, have significant and long-lasting psychological effects. Imagine for a moment that over the next few years, your physical appearance is going to change dramatically. You would become at least a head taller, gain anywhere from twenty to fifty pounds, and witness changes in your body proportions. Your voice would deepen, your muscular strength would increase, and hair would grow on body areas where it never previously existed. Your genitals would increase in size and become more sensitive to stimulation. You would have urges and feelings that you would only vaguely understand and would never have experienced before. Although some of these changes might be welcomed, others might evoke fear and embarrassment. They would certainly require a change in body image and self-concept. Your physical appearance would be substantially altered, leaving only a vague image of your former self. Others would respond to you differently and expect you to change your behavior acccordingly. Although the foregoing may seem exaggerated, it is precisely the process that every adolescent experiences. The psychological or behavioral adjustments caused by physical change are one major source of stress for the adolescent.

PREADOLESCENT DEVELOPMENT

To understand the physical changes that occur during adolescence, it is necessary to trace the course of development that precedes it. Human growth is a complex process. Development of various organ systems and body parts occurs at varying rates, each with its own pattern of growth. Growth, as measured in height and weight, is often used to illustrate the developmental process more simply. These measures roughly parallel development in other body areas. The first two years of life is a period of rapid growth. In that time, the average infant will almost double in height. From the child's third through fifth years, the rate of growth de-

11
Physical Growth and Maturation

celerates. In comparison to the first two years, growth is slower and more steady. Years six through seven represent a second growth spurt, which is rather mild in comparison to that of the first two years. Following year seven, a deceleration occurs again. Much like the quiet before the storm, growth slows to a steady and even rate that lasts until the advent of pubescence.

PUBESCENCE AND PUBERTY

Pubescence is a period of accelerated physical development, when body changes associated with sexual maturation occur. Pubescence precedes *puberty*, the period when sexual and reproductive capacity is attained. Although there is variation, females experience pubescence about one to two years before males. The average female begins pubescence at age ten, and puberty is usually achieved near the twelfth year. Puberty starts with the first menstrual period, when maximal physical growth is also observed. In contrast, males attain puberty, marked by the first ejaculation, between the ages of thirteen and fourteen.

It is believed that hormones secreted by the *anterior pituitary glands* located at the base of the brain trigger the sequence of changes that occur during pubescence. *Gonadotropic* and *corticotropic* hormones produced by the anterior pituitary gland act on the *gonads* (male and female organs of reproduction) and the *adrenal cortex*. Through a series of complex hormonal interactions, *androgens* and *estrogens* (male and female sex hormones) are produced. De-

12
NORMAL DEVELOPMENT OF THE ADOLESCENT

velopment of primary and secondary sex characteristics is stimulated, and the production of mature ova and sperm occurs. Related changes occur in nonsexual physiological functions and in body size, weight, and proportions.

Primary Sex Characteristics

The *primary sex characteristics* include the external genitals and the internal organs involved in reproduction. They are the most obvious distinguishing characteristics of males and females. Prior to pubescence, the development of the sex organs is slow in relation to that of other parts of the body. This situation reverses during adolescence, when the rate of change in the size of the sex organs is greater than that for height and weight. For example, the male *testes* may more than double in volume between the ages of thirteen and fifteen. The length and circumference of the *penis* may increase from 30 to 50 percent. The rapid growth of the genitals takes on special significance for the adolescent boy, who may equate genital size with potency and virility. Precocious development may lead to a false sense of masculinity, whereas late development may be associated with shame, embarrassment, or feelings of inferiority. It should be realized that there are great individual differences in the rate of development. Adults must be sensitive to the needs of children whose development deviates from the norm.

The initiation of *menstruation* is usually viewed as a sign of female sexual development. It may have important emotional consequences for the developing female. This depends on the age of onset and the young woman's degree of preparation for this event. The unprepared female may be frightened, embarrassed, and confused by this process. Additionally, menstruation is sometimes accompanied by unpleasant physical symptoms. For the adolescent and parent, menstruation may take on the importance of denoting the transition to physical sexual maturity and the attainment of reproductive capacity. It has been compared to the first male ejaculation as a sign of sexual maturity. Early or late onset of menstruation relative to the peer group can have the same psychological impact on the female as outer genital development can have on the male. The parents' attitudes toward sex, their acceptance of sexuality on the part of their child, and their ability to discuss sexual matters openly and honestly seriously affect the female adolescent's psychological reaction to the initiation of menstruation.

Secondary Sex Characteristics

Rapid development of secondary sex characteristics occurs in adolescence. *Secondary sex characteristics* are the physical features not directly involved in sexual reproduction that differentiate males and females. These features include the more outward and observable signs of one's sexual identity: the breasts; pubic, facial, and body hair; voice and body shape. The development of these features is critically important to the maturing adolescent. They determine outward physical appearance and publicly define one's degree of sexual maturity. Society's definition of masculinity, femininity, and attractiveness strongly influences the adolescent's reaction to the development of secondary sex characteristics. For females, Western society places emphasis on breast development and the acquisition of a slender physique with slightly flaring and rounded hips. The development of *pubic hair* has positive connotations as a sign of sexual maturity. The development of facial and body hair is typically viewed as unattractive and unfeminine.

For males, emphasis is placed on the development of a slender, broad-shouldered, muscular physique. The development of pubic, facial, and body hair is an important sign of virility and sexual maturity. Facial and chest hair takes on particular importance, as it serves as a specific differentiating sign of developing masculinity. The deepening of the male voice during pubescence is another sign of masculinity.

Other Physical Changes

Numerous nonsexual physical changes of varying significance take place during adolescence. Enlargement occurs in the sweat- and oil-producing glands of the adolescent. The sweat glands around the genitals and armpits show greatest development and are responsible for body odor. Activation of the oil-producing glands, especially around the face, is related to the occurrence of acne. Acne is particularly bothersome because most adolescents view acne as detracting from personal appearance. The adolescent's strong interest in peer acceptance and in being attractive to the opposite sex stimulates a greater emphasis on grooming, cleanliness, and personal hygiene.

Significant increases in cardiac and respiratory capacity and physical strength take place during adolescence. Compared to the preadolescent child, the adolescent is capable of performing more vigorous and sustained physical activity. Males surpass females in physical strength and endurance during adolescence. This is due to (1) cultural factors that have traditionally placed greater emphasis on males developing athletic ability, (2) the greater opportunities males typically have had to participate in vigorous physical activity, and (3) actual physical differences between males and females in respiratory and cardiac capacity and upper-body musculature.

Important physical changes take place during adolescence. Physical growth is completed, and sexual maturity is attained. Self-concept is modified to accommodate a changed physique and new physical abilities. The timing and nature of physical changes will affect the individual psychologically. Other factors also influence adolescent personality development. What are these factors? How do they interact to determine personality? These questions are addressed in the following chapter.

chapter *3*

Personality Development

Sue is a ninth grader at a middle-class, suburban junior high school. She is the captain of her intramural basketball team, earns above-average grades, and is popular among her peers. She gets along well with her parents and experiences the usual sibling problems with her eight-year-old brother. Both of Sue's parents are college educated. Sue hopes to enter a private Eastern college upon graduation from high school. Sue experienced puberty about two years ago and is developing into an attractive young person. She has just begun dating and sees Phil, a tenth grader from a nearby high school.

Roger is an eleventh grader and attends a big-city high school. He is short for his age and looks more like a ninth grader. His father is an avid sports fan, and Roger has never been able to live up to his father's expectations in the area of athletics. Roger has a few male friends, is basically shy, and does not date. He is described by his teachers as lacking in self-confidence and maturity. He rarely participates in school activities and makes below-average grades. He has no plans regarding college and is looking forward to the day when he finishes high school and can get a job.

Jill attends the tenth grade in a small high school in the rural South. Her mother married at eighteen and was divorced at age twenty, shortly after Jill was born. Jill and her mother lived with relatives until Jill was five years old and her mother remarried. The stepfather is a farm laborer and works primarily during the summer. He hunts and fishes the rest of the year and pays little attention to Jill and his two natural daughters. Jill's mother has a fourth-grade education and does her best to keep the family together and make ends meet. Jill has shown little interest in academics and has been socially promoted through school. She matured early, has been sexually active for several years, and dates boys several years older than she. She participates in no school activities and displays open contempt for those who do.

Larry is in the twelfth grade and lives in a decaying urban ghetto. His father died several years ago. He has two older brothers who have left home and are working at a local factory. Larry and his mother live on Welfare and Social Security, and Larry works after school at a *fast-food restaurant. Larry has experienced some academic difficulties, but he is extremely motivated and has made above-average grades while in high school. Larry wants to go to college but will settle for a junior college if he cannot obtain a scholarship. He is interested in girls and would like to participate in sports, but he is too busy with his studies and his job to pay much attention to either.*

These case histories, though not of real people, portray four different individuals, each displaying distinct personalities. Sue is bright, self-assured, and well adjusted; thus adolescence is a positive experience for her. Roger's experience is just the opposite, as he is a disappointment to his father and to himself. He has a poor self-concept, which is reinforced by the reactions of peers and adults, so he has chosen to withdraw. His sole goal is to survive adolescence and get on with the next phase of his life. Jill comes from a chaotic and unstable family. Her emotional development has not kept pace with her rapid physical development. She considers herself an adult but responds in terms of what is immediately gratifying. To her way of thinking, there is no future; hence, the present is what matters. On the other hand, for Larry, the future is all-important. Adolescence is a period of acceptance of responsibility, self-denial, and hard work. Although he is missing out on some important adolescent experiences, Larry is extremely "goal oriented" and willing to sacrifice immediate gratification for future accomplishment.

Sue, Roger, Jill, and Larry clearly show differing personalities. Experiential, environmental, economic, social, familial, geographic, and genetic factors, as well as a myriad of other variables, have interacted to produce four unique personalities. They differ in many ways but are all bound by the fact that they are going through a particularly important phase of their development—a phase that will produce lasting effects. The present chapter focuses on several key factors that affect adolescent personality. We attempt to expose the myths and misconceptions regarding adolescent personality and to clarify the conflicting ideas about this period.

WHAT IS PERSONALITY?

Personality is such a complex concept that its definition is still debated among psychologists. Theorists typically define personality in terms of the causes and determinants of behavior. A widely accepted definition, and one that we find particularly satisfying, defines personality in terms of the individual's enduring patterns of behavior. *Personality is how the individual behaves* or, in other words, the sum total of a person's behavior. It encompasses all the individual's habitual behaviors and includes both overt (external) and covert (internal) behaviors. It is measured and evaluated in terms of the individual's observable behaviors. Feelings and thoughts (covert behaviors) are especially important in terms of how they are reflected in specific actions. Personality traits are summary terms (labels) used to describe various commonly observed behavioral patterns. For example, the trait of shyness summarizes a behavioral pattern that may include withdrawal from interpersonal situations, anxiety in interpersonal situations, and reluctance to interact with strangers. Personality traits do not explain the causes of behavior; they merely serve as labels for observed behavior patterns.

Personality development begins at birth and continues throughout the entire life of the individual. We are continually changing, and experience constantly modifies existing personality. Experience shapes behavior and therefore determines personality. Not all experience has equal impact on personality. Some experiences have profound and long-lasting effects, whereas others have little or no significance. There are also enormous differences in how a specific event will affect different individuals. For example, how would each person from the previously described case studies react to receiving a D in English?

Interestingly, psychologists have long noted specific periods of life when certain experiences are critical to personality development. The presence or absence of certain experiences during these "critical periods" is believed to have long-lasting effects on behavior. Infancy, early childhood, and adolescence are commonly believed to be "critical periods" for personality development.

PREADOLESCENT PERSONALITY DEVELOPMENT

The child enters adolescence with a complex set of behavioral patterns that have been developing since birth. Some patterns are well established by adolescence and will persist into adulthood. Others are less stable and will undergo significant change because of adolescent experiences. The case histories of Sue, Roger, Jill, and Larry reveal little regarding their preadolescent experiences. However, it is obvious that they are of differing backgrounds and most likely have had differing preadolescent experiences. Sue, brought up in a "typical" middle-class environment, has already acquired a sense of responsibility and a positive attitude toward education. She has also developed the prerequisite social skills that enable her to interact positively with others. Jill, on the other hand, is the product of an unstable, lower-class home environment. Her environment has stressed day-to-day survival as opposed to planning for the future. Academic achievement has never been deemed important. The lack of a stable male figure at home has shaped her attitudes toward men. Her ideas regarding the roles of women in society have clearly been affected by her interactions with her mother. Hence, Sue and Jill enter adolescence with differing attitudes and personalities. For this reason, adolescent experiences will have varying effects on each of them and will further modify their developing patterns of behavior.

THEORIES OF ADOLESCENT PERSONALITY

At the beginning of this chapter, case histories were presented of four distinct personalities. On the surface, each differed—in terms of present behaviors, goals, and aspirations. The one commonality is that they are all adolescents. Is there something about all of them being adolescent that binds them together? Are there, in fact, experiences, feelings, and emotions common to the adolescent period?

At the beginning of this century, most scholars and experts on adolescence would have answered the foregoing questions affirmatively. G. Stanley Hall, one of the first psychologists to deal with adolescence as a unique period of human development, developed a theory of adolescence that was strongly influenced by the writings of Darwin. Hall viewed adolescent development and behavior as being controlled by universal genetic determinants. Environmental influences were largely ignored, and behavioral descriptions tended to minimize individual differences. Later, Arnold Gesell provided a year-by-year description of child and adolescent behavior. He described specific behavioral characteristics of each age. Erik Erikson, in his theory of the eight stages of man, identifies specific developmental crises that occur at each human stage of development. He views the manner in which each crisis is resolved as being critical to personality development. Universal stages of cognitive and moral development have been proposed by Jean Piaget and Lawrence Kohlberg, respectively.

Modern psychological theory places greater emphasis on environmental determinants of behavior rather than on universal aspects of behavior. Social and cultural influences are stressed over strictly predetermined genetic influences. The nature of our rapidly changing, culturally diverse society makes it difficult to offer conclusive statements regarding any group of individuals. Some theorists have even challenged the concept of adolescence as a distinct period of development. They view development as a continuous process from birth to death and deny that adolescence is, in itself, a unique period of growth.

A cautious, middle-of-the-road view appears best. It is felt that adolescence is a unique period of development, although specific experiences are not universal. Cultural and environmental factors strongly influence each adolescent's behavior and personality. Certain commonalities among adolescents do exist, and within the limits of current knowledge, general statements can be made regarding adolescent personality.

The Storm and Stress Theory

A popular view of adolescence portrays it as a period of "storm and stress." Experts have described adolescents as inconsistent, unpredictable, erratic, emotional, and self-centered. Adolescents have been portrayed as incapable of self-criticism, out of touch with reality, and conflict-ridden. A classic picture of adolescence is found in Shakespeare's *Romeo and Juliet*, where we see the irrational passions, emotionality, impulsivity, and family conflict that have come to characterize the popular conception of adolescence.

Hollywood and Broadway have presented various stereotyped and sometimes superficial views of adolescence that fit the popular conception. *West Side Story* gives us a view of adolescent behavior within an urban ghetto, where gang warfare and delinquency are superimposed against a background of adolescent love and emotion. Adult authority figures are held in contempt and subject to ridicule. The concept of delinquents suffering from a "social disease" is satirized.

The *Impossible Years*, a Broadway comedy and movie

of the sixties, pictures the trials and tribulations of a psychiatrist raising a teenage daughter. Its title speaks for itself. The movies *Woodstock* and *Hair* make explicit statements regarding adolescent mores and values of the 1960s and early 1970s. *Hair* provides a view of an adolescent subculture characterized by drug use, rebellion against adult authority, and peer-group solidarity.

Experts and mass media alike have traditionally portrayed adolescents as behaving in ways that would indicate emotional disturbance (at other periods in life). Psychoanalysts, including Anna Freud, daughter of Sigmund Freud, suggest that an adolescent not showing adjustment problems may in fact be developing abnormally. We are left with the impression that the adolescent is expected to be emotionally unstable and that the essence of the period is emotional conflict.

G. Stanley Hall applied the phrase "storm and stress" to adolescence in the early 1900s and set the pattern for much of our contemporary thought regarding adolescent personality. For Hall, the adolescent's personality is a series of contradictions. The adolescent vacillates between periods of enthusiasm, high energy, and elation and periods of depression, apathy, and inertia. In modern psychological terminology, such an individual might be labeled as having a manic-depressive personality. Hall believed the adolescent was stricken with conflicting traits of selfishness and altruism, sensitivity and callousness, vanity and humility. No wonder Hall viewed adolescence as a period of "storm and stress"! Hall saw turmoil during adolescence as a universal and inevitable consequence of normal human development. Everyone had to go through this period to develop into a "normal" adult. Parents and educators were asked to be tolerant and accepting of the adolescent's eccentricities. Little could be done about them, anyway! Reassuringly, the storm and stress of adolescence would inevitably be followed by adult maturity.

Hall's position remains controversial, and various aspects of it have been widely criticized. Anthropologists studying other cultures have taken Hall to task over his belief in the universal nature of adolescent conflict. They point to various non-Western cultures where the adolescent experience differs greatly from that in the West. Anthropologists cite numerous cultures where adolescent personality appears to be tension and conflict free. Criticisms aside (and there are many), there remain many adherents to Hall's singular definition of adolescence as a period of anxiety and psychological turmoil. There is considerable evidence to support this view and numerous studies that refute it.

Albert Bandura, a noted behavioral psychologist, is a vocal critic of the "storm and stress" picture of adolescence. He and other behavioral psychologists suggest that there is nothing unique about the adolescent period that should make it more conflict-ridden than any other stage of life. They believe that there are many "myths" concerning adolescent personality, and much of their research is directed toward "exposing" these myths.

As mentioned, it is popularly believed that parent–child conflict intensifies during adolescence. Parents and adolescents are typically pictured as adversaries, frequently struggling over independence, style of dress, or selection of friends. The image generated by the previously mentioned

Impossible Years fits this stereotype. Research by Bandura and others suggests that the notion of parent–child conflict is greatly exaggerated. They find that family ties remain strong during adolescence and that most adolescents actually adopt, rather than reject, parental values and attitudes. They find that parents generally approve of peer associations. Parent–child relations are pictured as warm and supportive. Bandura accuses the mass media and mental health professionals of perpetuating the "mythology" regarding adolescence. He accuses the mass media of sensationalizing deviant adolescent behavior, thereby creating—in the mind of the public—the impression that such behavior represents the typical adolescent. This observation is certainly well founded. When was the last time you saw a movie or TV program that portrayed adolescence as anything other than a period of conflict and stress?

Bandura's point about mental health professionals is also well taken. In our clinical practice, most adolescent referrals are troubled and experiencing family problems. We see runaways, school dropouts, delinquents, and adolescents from broken homes. Many show severe emotional problems, and almost all fit the popular stereotype. Working daily with such adolescents tends to cloud our perspective regarding normal adolescent personality. Clinical experience may cause the mental health professional to generalize the adolescent experience inaccurately. The important point is that adolescence, like other developmental periods, involves uniquely satisfying as well as frustrating experiences.

TIMING OF SEXUAL MATURITY
AND PERSONALITY

Most of us have noted differences in behavior and personality between early and late sexual maturers. In every junior high school, we see the greatly admired eighth- or ninth-grade male who is athletic, muscular and "mature." There is also the physically mature junior-high female, who is often viewed less favorably by her peers than her early-maturing male counterpart.

Several interesting research studies have examined the effect of early and late sexual maturation in Western society. The onset of sexual maturity affects males and females differently. Most *early-maturing boys* are popular with their peers and tend to be social and athletic leaders. They are perceived as leaders and often demonstrate more adultlike behavior, primarily because they are treated more like adults. On the other hand, *early-maturing girls* are comparatively unpopular with their peers. These individuals are considered precocious and sexually aggressive within the peer group. As a result of early physical development, early-maturing girls are often exposed to many situations for which they are not physically or socially prepared. This creates a considerable amount of stress, so that adjustment may be impeded for these individuals.

Late-maturing boys often feel inferior because of their smaller, underdeveloped physiques. Shyness and social withdrawal are considered frequent side effects of delayed male maturation. These individuals are often rejected by their female peers, who tend to favor the early-maturing boys. Thus, the peer group inadvertently encourages immature behavior patterns by limiting opportunities for mature social interaction. Unlike late-maturing boys, their female counterparts are generally well accepted by their peers. The "nice girl" connotation is often observed because of the typical lack of social and sexual aggressiveness. However, these individuals usually express dissatisfaction with the tendency to be treated like children.

As for the long-term effects of the timing of sexual maturation on personality, the research is speculative and inconclusive. There is some evidence of mixed effects for both early and late maturers, each experiencing certain advantages and disadvantages. For example, early-maturing males were found to hold leadership roles more often; yet they were also considered more impulsive and self-indulgent. The early-maturing males were more successful vocationally; however, they were less socially active. Research concerning long-term effects for females suggests the perpetuation of those characteristics that are developed as a result of early or late maturation. Again, the speculation on these long-term effects should be taken with a grain of salt. Personality is constantly changing and is unlikely to be permanently molded by the experience of early or late maturation.

SELF-CONCEPT AND IDENTITY

In an adolescent psychology course taught by one of the authors, students were given the assignment of writing an essay answering the question "Who am I?" These college students were in the unique position of studying a period that they were experiencing. Many students were perplexed by this seemingly simple assignment. One young man wrote:

> I am Frederick Norton, age nineteen. I am a sophomore and live in Newmark dorm. I think this is what you want. You want to know "who am I." Right? I thought I knew the answer. But now it's not so clear. Things were simpler before coming to college. My home is Duck Hill, population 800. Everyone knew me there, so of course I knew who I was. I had my whole life mapped out, or at least my parents did. Pre-med, the whole thing. Hated Chem 101, almost flunked. Some pre-med student! I'm not sure who I am or what I really want to do with my life. I like sociology, psych's not bad either. But this is not telling you who I am. My girl friend Gloria says I'm moody and have no sense of humor. She says I take things too seriously. Maybe so. Dad and I don't agree on many things anymore. Mom's real proud of me. Tells all her friends about my A's in philosophy and history. She never mentioned the D in chemistry. Heck, I don't know who I am. But I'm working on it.

A nineteen-year-old woman stated:

> My name is Tracy Starner. I am nineteen years old. I am five feet, three inches tall and have long brown hair. My parents live in Dallas, Texas. I am the middle of

three children. I have an older brother and younger sister. I enjoy tennis and waterskiing. My major is mathematics, and I would like to teach one day. I am a warm and sensitive person and enjoy being around people.

Another female student wrote:

I am me!

We all perceive ourselves in different ways. As just illustrated, perceptions range from the confused to the overly simplistic to the disarmingly simple. The way in which people perceive themselves is known as *self-concept.*

One of the most critical aspects of adolescent personality is the development of the self-concept. The adolescent's perceptions of his or her body, behavior, attitudes, thoughts, and emotions constitute the self-concept and vitally affect the adjustment and general well-being of the individual. Self-concept is a difficult entity to define because of its intangible, metaphysical, and ever-changing qualities. However, many psychologists feel that self-concept is useful in attempting to understand adolescent behavior.

The self-concept of the newborn is characterized by oneness with the mother. The infant is unable to differentiate the attributes of the mother from those of the self. As sensory and cognitive development unfolds, the child grows to view the self in a very "egocentric" manner. The perception of the self is vastly unrelated to external cues; hence the perceptions of the self are generated by that person. During early and middle adolescence, however, the self-concept is largely based upon cues that emanate from external sources. Social interactions serve as an important testing ground and source of feedback that critically affect self-concept development.

Closely associated with self-concept is Erik Erikson's term *identity*. Erikson contends that a major developmental task of adolescence is the establishment of a personal identity (i.e., a secure sense of self or self-concept). He divides the human life span into eight stages, each involving a specific crisis. The crisis of adolescence is *Identity vs. Identity Diffusion*. The manner in which the adolescent resolves this crisis is, for Erikson, critical to healthy personality development.

Suggestive of Hall's concept of "storm and stress" is Erikson's theory that every adolescent will go through the struggle of establishing a personal identity. This struggle stems in part from the need to redefine self-concept following the rapid physiological changes that accompany puberty. The newfound sexuality, the requirements of a changed social role, and new behavioral expectations force the young person to question all the rules and regulations that previously guided behavior. The old attitudes and values must be modified in light of the changed circumstances of the adolescent. The adolescent is in a struggle to maintain a stable self-concept in the face of constant change. The crisis involves maintaining emotional stability within an environment that promotes confusion.

Erikson speaks of identity diffusion, which he sees as being "temporarily unavoidable" during adolescence. However, failure to resolve the problem of confused identity may result in serious psychological problems in which the sense of self is distorted, volatile, and unstable.

Although this view is largely theoretical and without substantial empirical (scientific) support, we have observed evidence of identity crises in some adolescents. Often, rebelliousness, self-glorification, confusion, and anxiety, among other symptoms, are partially attributable to a diffuse and unstable identity. Compensation, for adolescents, usually takes the form of total identification with well-defined groups that are characteristically intolerant of others. Examples of these include social cliques, clubs, gangs, and religious cults. With maturity, these needs to identify completely with others diminish. The internal references again take on more importance in the development of the self-concept.

Self-esteem or self-worth is also a vital aspect in self-concept development. Feelings of self-worth are determined by an individual's evaluation of his or her daily social experiences. The individual's self-esteem is critical in formulating important decisions pertaining to such areas as career, marriage, morality, health, and religion. Although influenced by personality, positive self-esteem is usually stimulated in an atmosphere of encouragement, support, and approval.

ADOLESCENT ADJUSTMENT

More than anything else, adolescence is a period of adjustment. We have discussed various factors that influence adolescent personality and have noted that each individual experiences adolescence in a unique way. For some, adolescence is a period of "storm and stress," with one crisis following the other. For others, the establishment of a personal identity occupies much of the period. As we have previously noted, children bring to adolescence a developing personality. Some are more prepared than others to deal with the adjustments required during this time. The adolescent's success, or failure, in adjusting will have a profound effect upon future personality development.

Because of the rapid physical changes associated with puberty, the adolescent must adjust to a changed physique and new physical capabilities. This requires modification of self-concept and a readiness to accept these changes. If the changes coincide with those of the adolescent's peers, the adjustment will usually proceed smoothly. Changes that deviate from the norm may provoke behavioral difficulties. Our previous discussion concerning the effects of late and early maturation illustrates this point.

During late adolescence the individual must accept the fact that his or her changed physical appearance is now relatively permanent. The adolescent's perception of both positive and negative aspects of physical appearance becomes a part of self-image. Parental and peer-group emphasis of positive characteristics can promote healthy personality development despite physical deficiencies.

More important are the changed social expectations that accompany physical development. Society expects adolescents to be more mature and independent than children and to accept more responsibility and be more accountable for their actions. An adolescent's emotional maturity is expected to correspond to his or her level of physical maturity. Adjustment problems may arise when emotional maturity does not correlate with physical maturity.

As indicated in the previous chapter, physical sexual maturity is attained during adolescence. The adolescent must adjust to new feelings and emotions associated with sexuality. Relationships with the opposite sex change dramatically. Emotional maturity must accompany sexual maturity, and adults should foster a healthy attitude toward sex. Adolescent sexual experiences and the attitudes developed during this period will inexorably influence adult sexual expression. Adult sexual inadequacy has many times been traced to the adolescent period.

The final adjustment of adolescence involves preparation for the transition into adulthood. There are many tasks that the adolescent must accomplish to ensure a graceful transition. A level of emotional maturity must be attained that will allow the person to relinquish dependence on parents and assume an autonomous adult role. Preparation must be made for economic independence through training for a specific vocation or occupation. A level of independence, responsibility, and emotional maturity must be attained that will allow the individual to make intelligent decisions regarding marriage, family, or alternate lifestyles.

part **II**

CONFLICT
AND ADJUSTMENT

The purpose of this section is to explore areas of adolescent development that are particularly vulnerable to conflict. In a rapidly changing society, the outlines of expected behaviors become blurred for many adolescents. This is particularly true in the areas of sexual behavior and alcohol and drug use. These controversial topics focus on the unique historical and contemporary forces that influence adolescent decisions. Also presented are chapters on delinquency, suicide, and other mental-health-related problems that require special attention.

chapter **4**

Sexuality

React for a moment to the following terms that might be found on a word-association test evaluating sexual attitudes. Do these terms evoke positive, negative, or neutral reactions? What type of mental picture does each evoke?

Intercourse, premarital sex, homosexuality, masturbation, vagina, penis, fornication, oral sex, rape, prostitution, pornographic, erection, perversion, love.

Would you feel comfortable reading these words to your great aunt or uncle? What about defining them for a group of thirteen-year-olds?

No area of human behavior evokes more interest, discussion, controversy, and emotion than sexuality. From biblical proscriptions to modern-day humor, sexuality is an integral part of our lives. Newspaper columnists advise us about it, and films graphically depict it. Books that tell us "how to" and "everything we wanted to know about it" many times become overnight best-sellers. Sex can be a topic of both frivolous and serious discussion. Although researchers have provided us with a general understanding of the biological nature of sexuality, information about the emotional and interpersonal aspects of it is, at best, speculative.

The sex act is more than just a biological occurrence, and one's emotional response to it may range from a deeply felt sense of personal pleasure and satisfaction to one of revulsion and humiliation. Sexual relations may occur within a context ranging from loving, sharing, and giving to one that is purely exploitive. A human being's sense of his or her own sexuality is deeply personal and affects many other aspects of behavior. However, the expression of sexuality is strongly influenced by an interaction of social values, religious and moral beliefs, and legal codes. The study of human sexuality is extremely complex and fraught with much misinformation and misunderstanding.

We have previously defined adolescence as beginning when sexual maturity is reached and reproductive capacity is attained. Adolescence marks a milestone in one's biological sexual development. However, as we have tried to point out, the biological nature of sexuality is only a small part of one's sexual identity and sense of sexuality.

In looking at sexual development, we are actually looking at three interrelated areas of growth: physical sexual development, sex-role development, and development of psychological sexual maturity.

PHYSICAL SEXUAL DEVELOPMENT

The mechanics of physical sexual development have been discussed in Chapter 2. With the advent of puberty, the adolescent achieves the capacity to reproduce. An adult physique is acquired, with the corresponding development of secondary sex characteristics. Physical and hormonal changes greatly increase the adolescent's responsiveness to sexually arousing stimuli. Anecdotal reports regarding the adolescent male's ability to become sexually aroused at the most inopportune times are, by now, legendary. Thoughts and fantasies as well as more concrete forms of stimulation can cause sexual arousal. Nocturnal emissions accompanied by sexually arousing dreams are quite common during early adolescence.

Less is known about the sexual responsiveness of adolescent females. At one time, it was commonly believed that females did not become as easily aroused as males. Females were considered to be less responsive to visual stimulation and fantasy and to require more direct physical stimulation than males to become sexually aroused. This view has been challenged by some authorities who believe that previously observed differences in male–female sexual arousal patterns are due to social and cultural factors more than to physiological factors. Society's "double standard" reinforced the view that females were less sexually responsive than males. "Nice girls" were not supposed to be concerned with sexual matters or obtain enjoyment from sex. The male played the role of aggressor, and the female was cast in a more passive, nonassertive role. The fact is, adolescent females can and certainly do become sexually aroused. Once aroused, they display patterns of sexual responsiveness that closely parallel male patterns.

SEX-ROLE DEVELOPMENT

Thus, with the advent of puberty, the individual has attained the capacity to reproduce and respond sexually. From a social and behavioral view, sexual development begins in early infancy and, like personality development, never ceases. The development of one's sexual identity, one's sense of "maleness" or "femaleness," and the adoption of sex-appropriate behavior are critical to the manner in which one adjusts sexually during adolescence and adulthood.

We recognize the inherent difficulty of dealing with concepts that are difficult if not impossible to define. Terms such as *maleness, femaleness,* and *sex-appropriate* mean different things to different people. Rapid social change has blurred the line between traditional male- and female-stereotype role behaviors and has led to a greater acceptance of alternative sex roles and life-styles. To understand our dilemma better, define for yourself *maleness, femaleness,* and *sex-appropriate.* What does it mean psychologically and socially to be male or female? Are there behaviors that one can precisely define as being distinctly characteristic of either sex? If there are, what factors determine such behaviors?

Gender is determined at the moment of conception. Following birth and until puberty, social and cultural factors play a prominent role in the development of sexual identity and sex-appropriate behavior. In obvious and sometimes quite subtle ways, boys are taught to "act like boys" and girls, to "act like girls." The conditioning process starts early and continues through adolescence. Physiological differences are minor and have very little effect upon behavior.

To understand the effects of experience on sex-role development, let us take the example of Billy and Donna. Their experiences, though not universal, illustrate how the conditioning process works.

> *Three-day-old Donna is brought home from the hospital in a cute pink outfit. Grandma affixes a pink ribbon to Donna's hair. Dad gives Donna a kiss on the cheek and tells her how pretty she is. Grandpa calls her his little angel. A neighbor drops by with a doll for Donna. Donna cries when she is wet, and everyone comments on how clean and ladylike she already is.*

> *Two-month-old Billy Jr. is being readied for a family outing. He kicks and screams in his bath, and mother thinks aloud—"Well, boys will be boys." Dad can't wait to see Billy Jr. in his new New York Yankee T-shirt. Finally ready to leave, Dad picks up Billy Jr. and says "Let's go, little man, we don't want to be late."*

Donna is celebrating her second birthday. The cake on the dining table is decorated with yellow flowers and three miniature ballerinas. After singing happy birthday, Donna sets about opening her gifts. They include a nurse's kit, a set of miniature pots and pans, a miniature tea set, a dollhouse, and a Cinderella storybook.

The scene at Billy Jr.'s second birthday differs dramatically. Billy Jr.'s interest in cowboys and Indians is reflected everywhere. His cowboy suit and boots fit perfectly. Atop his birthday cake sit three cowboys on horseback. The gifts reflect Billy Jr.'s "all-boy" image. They include a doctor's kit, a dump truck, a ball and bat, a set of electric trains, and a Davy Crockett storybook.

The story can go on and on. Conditioning is a subtle process that constantly encourages adolescents to assume the "appropriate" sex role.

At age four Donna begins taking dance lessons, and Billy accompanies his father on his first camping trip. At age eight Donna signs up for Brownies, and Billy is enrolled in Little League. At all ages, both Donna and Billy Jr. observe the interaction of their parents and other significant adults. Dad mows the lawn while Mom vacuums the carpet. Most of Billy Jr.'s elementary-school teachers are female; the school principal is male. Donna's minister, a male, delivers the sermon on Sunday; the church ladies prepare and serve the supper that follows.

By the time Billy Jr. and Donna reach adolescence, each will have developed a sense of his or her sexual identity. Both will know almost "instinctively" what it means to be male or female. Their best friends and confidants will most likely be of their own sex. Although there may be some minor flirtations with members of the opposite sex, they will typically fall back on their same-sex peers for companionship or support. Billy Jr. and Donna have been conditioned to assume traditional roles.

Experiences during adolescence will most likely continue to reinforce "sex-appropriate" behaviors. Family, friends, and society at large will hold different behavioral expectations for Billy Jr. and for Donna. Behaviors at variance with societal expectations will likely meet with strong disapproval.

PSYCHOLOGICAL SEXUAL MATURATION

The individual enters adolescence with a sense of his or her sex-role identity and with an emerging capacity to reproduce. Hormonal and other physical changes allow the adolescent to be sexually aroused by various types of stimulation. Some authorities believe that a sex drive is established that directs behavior and requires gratification through sexual behavior. Though the term *drive* has been overused in psychology and is greatly misunderstood, it may, for illustrative purposes, help us understand what the adolescent experiences. Through the ability to become sexually aroused, the adolescent discovers a new way to derive pleasure and personal physical satisfaction. In effect, the adolescent has acquired a new "toy." Obviously, this is no ordinary "toy," for it carries significant psychological implications. The typical young adolescent fails to understand its significance and focuses solely on the physical nature of sexuality. Sexuality for the early adolescent is generally devoid of the concept of love and adult emotion; rather, it is usually approached in an egocentric and self-gratifying manner. In terms of psychological sexual maturity, the young adolescent is at the stage of "physical sexuality." Little else should be expected. Cognitive psychologists have shown us that young adolescents have a limited ability to deal with abstract concepts. Concepts such as interpersonal sexual love and affection are beyond the cognitive level of understanding for the typical adolescent. The early adolescent lacks the experience and emotional maturity to think and behave on such a level.

The adolescent's newly discovered sexuality spurs an interest in sexual matters and may lead to sexual experimentation. Although attitudes are changing, the topic of sex remains taboo in many homes. Where it is discussed, discussions are likely to center around the do's and don't's, and many topics are strictly off limits. Parents and adolescents often find it difficult to accept one another's sexuality. Discussions of sex lack the personal and emotional quality needed to convey the meaning of mature adult sexuality. Sex education at home is often characterized as "too little, too late."

Adolescents are curious about sex and acquire most of their information and misinformation about it outside the home. Information is passed from one age group to the next in a manner similar to the way in which rules and regulations of street games are conveyed from one generation to the next.

Masturbation

As previously noted, the sexual behavior of the young adolescent is experimental and exploratory. The two most frequent causes of the first ejaculation in males are nocturnal emission and masturbation. An overwhelming majority of boys masturbate sometime during adolescence, and for many, this practice continues into adulthood. There are less data regarding girls, but masturbation is common among females, though it occurs at a lower rate than for males. For the vast majority of adolescents, masturbation can be practiced without any detrimental physical or psychological effects. It occurs at such high rates that it should be viewed as normal behavior. In early adolescence, where outlets for sexual expression are extremely limited, masturbation frequently provides the only legitimate sexual outlet.

The most frequently observed negative effect of masturbation is the feeling of guilt that may be associated with it. Masturbation is rarely, if ever, discussed with parents and is certainly not viewed as a topic of "polite" conversation. Although it is a common occurrence during adolescence, adults are quite reluctant to admit that they have ever engaged in such behavior. The impression acquired by many adolescents is that masturbation is something "dirty" and something to be "ashamed of." It is basically viewed as a taboo, secret behavior engaged in without the knowledge of one's parents and other adults. Many adolescents are left with the impression that they are doing something wrong, shameful, and abnormal. The mythology regarding the detrimental effects of masturbation (blindness and acne), no matter how ludicrous it appears to adults, may be taken seriously by the more naive adolescent. The problem with such guilt is that it may adversely affect the adolescent's attitude toward sex. Masturbation is usually the first encounter the adolescent has with sex and may immediately become associated with guilt and shame. Hardly a positive introduction to sexuality!

Some argue that masturbation, if engaged in excessively, may result in a detrimental attitude toward sex. An attitude may develop that regards sex as an act purely for personal pleasure and self-gratification. Regard for its interpersonal aspects may fail to develop. Although such is possible, it is believed that excessive masturbation is a symptom of social maladjustment rather than a cause. In our clinical experience, we have found that individuals who employ masturbation as their primary sexual outlet may show maladjustment in various other areas. They may employ masturbation as a result of their inability to form relationships that would result in the availability of other forms of sexual expression.

Adolescent Homosexual Experience

Homosexual experiences also occur among adolescents, especially males, and may be part of some adolescents' normal psychological sexual development. A differentiation should be made between homosexuality that occurs during adolescence and that which occurs among adult homosexuals. Adolescent homosexuality is far removed from adult homosexuality. For the early adolescent, homosexual behavior is exploratory and occurs primarily because of the absence of available opposite-sex partners. Like masturbation, adolescent homosexuality represents a way of satisfying a sex drive for which there are few legitimate outlets. It involves few of the intimacies of adult homosexuality and may involve group and mutual masturbation. For males, this behavior has a heterosexual orientation in that the discussions and fantasies expressed during adolescent homosexual activities usually involve relations with the opposite sex. The participants rarely consider their behavior homosexual, and emotional attachments to partners rarely develop.

Like masturbation, adolescent homosexual experiences are rarely of significant long-term consequence. The vast majority of adolescents soon end this type of behavior and move on to heterosexual activities. Less frequently, the homosexual behavior does persist and may eventually be followed by the assumption of a homosexual life-style. However, no convincing cause-and-effect relationship has been established between adolescent homosexual experiences and adult homosexuality.

Adolescent Heterosexual Experience

Paralleling masturbation and homosexual activities is a growing interest in the opposite sex. Unlike masturbation and homosexual activity, relations with the opposite sex have both *social* and *sexual* consequences. Heterosexual patterns vary among adolescents according to a number of variables such as social background, geographic location, and age. This makes it difficult to offer specific statements about the development of heterosexual behavior that apply to all adolescents. In general, early heterosexual encounters center around school-related activities. These may include attending school dances, football games, and other similar social functions. Flirting with classmates is common. In junior high and high school, class parties where boys and girls arrive and leave with their same-sex friends are common. During such functions a limited amount of pairing off may occur. Dating typically begins during this period. Early sexual experiences are usually limited to occasional petting. Crushes may develop, and the ritual of "going steady" is observed.

From a social view, males and females learn to interact and relate in new ways. They acquire new sets of behaviors and learn the rules and regulations appropriate for heterosexual activities. Early heterosexual activities can be likened to the sparring that takes place during the beginning rounds of a boxing match—each boxer anxiously testing out the other, trying to judge the opponent's reactions and adjust his or her own style accordingly. One of the authors worked at a summer camp a number of years ago and had an opportunity to observe closely the heterosexual activities of thirteen- and fourteen-year-olds. Males and females interacted with each other in various activities during the day, but evening socials brought about entirely different types of behavior. Teenage friends of the opposite sex approached each other anxiously and nervously. Conversations were stilted, and everyone appeared awkward in their new social environment.

From these early heterosexual encounters, adolescents gain valuable experience in social interaction. They become more relaxed around the opposite sex and learn to "be themselves." As the adolescent gets older, relationships generally become more serious, intense, and emotionally charged. The beginnings of mature adult sexuality emerge.

During middle and late adolescence, sexual experimentation continues. Sexual intercourse may occur in a variety of contexts, from casual "one-night stands" to more enduring relationships. Sexual expression remains rather egocentric, although sexual relations occur more frequently in the context of emotional relationships with other individuals.

One of the most controversial facets of sexual development is premarital sex, and arguments can be made both for and against adolescent sexual experimentation. On the negative side, adolescents who are emotionally unprepared for such activities may feel guilt or shame about their behavior. The adolescent may feel exploited by his or her partner or develop attitudes toward sex that ignore its emotional aspects. The possibility of pregnancy is always present, as is the possibility of contracting venereal disease.

Although we are not advocates of premarital sexual relations among adolescents, there are certain instances where such experiences may be positive. Religious and moral questions aside, premarital sexual experiences may aid the adolescent in developing a mature understanding of sexuality. If sexual relations occur in a context of respect and mutual sharing, the adolescent can gain valuable insights into the emotional nature of sexuality. The adolescent may also learn about his or her sexual responsiveness as well as that of the partner. Premarital sexual experiences may provide a means for learning about and testing one's sexuality. A degree of sexual experience and sophistication prior to marriage may, for some, enhance adjustment to the sexual demands of marriage. Finally, many proponents of premarital sex maintain that social rules discouraging sexual experimentation are simply artificial and unhealthy restraints upon our most natural drives.

When the individual is able to combine psychologically love and physical sexuality, psychological sexual maturity is reached. The age at which this happens varies greatly.

The topic of human sexuality is complex and controversial. Individual differences are reflected in the course and manner of each person's sexual development. Various factors will affect individual sexual development and the manner in which sexuality is expressed. What we have outlined should not be taken as a universal model for normal sexual development. Rather, our purpose is to illustrate the interaction of physical sexual development, sex-role development, and psychological sexual development. Adolescents are dynamic people, constantly experimenting, exploring, and learning from their experiences. There is much for the adolescent to learn in the area of sexuality. The adult's role is to foster healthy attitudes and teach the adolescent to view sex in a mature and responsible way. As with any new learning experience, the adolescent is likely to stumble at times and make errors. Adults must learn to accept such errors and deal openly with the challenge of adolescent sexuality.

Continued dialogue between adolescents and adults regarding sexual matters can foster healthy sexual adjustment and minimize problems. Adults must accept that adolescents have sexual needs and that sexual experimentation is part of normal development. The transitory nature of this period of growth is exemplified by adolescent sexual development. If all goes well, the individual will emerge from adolescence with a mature concept of sexuality.

chapter 5

Alcohol
and Drugs:
Use and Abuse

Many people associate the increased drug use among youths with the social and political activism of the 1960s and early 1970s. Marijuana and LSD are often viewed as integral parts of the youth scene, which included sit-ins, rock music concerts, and antiwar protests. Although much of the restlessness and dissatisfaction with conventional society has diminished, drug and alcohol use continues to increase at a frightening rate. Approximately three-fourths of all adolescents drink alcohol, and about one-fourth of this group are considered problem drinkers. Although the figures vary, it is estimated that half of older adolescents smoke marijuana at least occasionally. Use of narcotics, depressants (other than alcohol), and hallucinogens (other than marijuana) is observed less frequently.

It has often been said that we are living in a culture obsessed with the ingestion of chemicals. Caffeine is used to perk up; sleeping "aids" are used to wind down; tranquilizers "calm the nerves"; and stimulants increase activity and reduce appetite. Marijuana is smoked to heighten the senses, and alcohol is used to dull them. Chemicals are socially (and medically) prescribed for virtually every imaginable mood and activity.

These facts became more apparent after the surge of attention given youths who began experimenting with relatively unfamiliar and novel substances (e.g., marijuana and LSD). The severe criticism of these new patterns of drug use was countered with the assertion that these substances represented a less dangerous alternative to alcohol. Marijuana was symbolic of the "antiestablishment" trends that expressed opposition to traditional social conventions, including alcohol consumption.

Although the "alternative" theory of drug use remains a hotly debated issue, many youths accurately assessed the potential danger of alcohol. This drug is far and away more abused than any other substance. Alcohol abuse is implicated in a large number of teenage accident-related deaths, homicides, thefts, and suicides. More deaths, injuries, and destruction of property can be attributed to alcohol use than to that of all other drugs combined. There is some irony in the fact that the most potentially dangerous drug, alcohol, is also the most widely available and accepted drug.

CAUSES

The causes and reasons for the developing pattern of drug use are legion. Although adolescents are usually not fully aware of the reasons for their decisions to use certain chemicals, we believe that several common factors explain the onset of drug use by many adolescents.

First, alcohol or drug use is viewed as instrumental in achieving several goals. Common goals include (1) acceptance into peer groups, (2) being perceived as knowledgeable or "cool," (3) satisfaction of curiosity, and/or (4) mood alteration. Whatever the goal is, ingestion of a particular chemical may help to achieve it. Successful achievement of various goals through drug use sets the stage for excessive dependence on these chemicals. Initially, drug intake is a means to another end. Later, this process becomes the end in itself.

Second, drug use (and later abuse) has its roots in the tendency to ingest chemicals as a short-term method of dealing with personal stress. The novice drinker often discovers that alcohol reduces anxiety in social settings. The marijuana user finds temporary relief from boredom through the novel perceptions that are produced by the drug. A college student fights fatigue during final exam week by taking amphetamines. Abusive habits are often based upon the use of drugs as a temporary, chemical solution to problems that are better managed through changes in attitude, behavior, and life-style.

Third, many adolescents begin using drugs (particularly nicotine and alcohol) to lay claim to a more mature status. These drugs are used as an expression of independence and maturity. A "devil-may-care" attitude concerning drugs is too often perceived as masculine and adultlike. Certain styles of smoking or drinking are frequently meant to appear feminine and seductive.

Fourth, the use of drugs or alcohol is perceived as an important expression of group solidarity for adolescents. Use of particular substances promotes group cohesion in many cases and helps to distinguish those who are "in" from those who are "out." Often the cohesive group of teenagers who use drugs such as marijuana or cocaine may be expressing opposition to social conventions. This is, in part, caused by the need for peer-group solidarity and an increasing need for independence. It appears that every generation of this century has expressed opposition, in various proscribed manners, to the values of the older generation. Drug use has played an increasingly prominent role in this expression of rebellion.

As mentioned, there are numerous causes of drug and alcohol use. Whatever the reasons, the physical and social consequences assume greater importance and visibility as drug use progresses. With many substances, there are risks of overdose, addiction, tissue damage, and marked undesirable behavior change. Social consequences of using chemicals may be more damaging than the physiological effects. Possible social and legal consequences of drug use include imprisonment, divorce, impoverishment, alienation, or rejection. Society has assumed a very punitive and ineffective approach to curtailing the use of hard drugs (particularly narcotics). Society punishes the drug user, whose problems are primarily of a social, medical, and psychological nature. Legal sanctions have also created the opportunity for tremendous profits from drug trafficking, thus establishing an incentive for dealers to increase markets by finding new users. The price of narcotics becomes so exorbitant that the addicted users squander all their financial resources on drugs. Inevitably, many users must turn to stealing or prostitution or must themselves deal in drugs to maintain their habits. Drug abusers have been more ineptly and callously managed by society than any other group of individuals with medical problems except, perhaps, the mentally ill. Drug addiction is a disease that may be cured by professional treatment—a prescription not yet fully recognized by our criminal justice system or by society as a whole.

To aid in the understanding of drug use and abuse, the major categories of drugs that are commonly misused are discussed in terms of their legal, social, behavioral, and physiological aspects.

DEPRESSANTS

Depressant drugs include a number of chemicals that have a common effect—they depress the central nervous system. Alcohol, barbiturates, and tranquilizers are major categories of depressants, and many types of chemicals are represented in each category.

Alcohol

Alcohol is the oldest depressant in terms of use and the most pervasive in terms of abuse. Most people are inclined not to think of alcohol as a drug, or especially as a *danger-*

ous drug, because of its widespread social acceptance. Alcohol abuse accounts for a large part of health costs in the United States. There are an estimated 10 million alcoholics in this country alone. It is impossible to put a price tag on the human suffering, anguish, and despair caused by alcoholism. As mentioned, one in four teenagers has a drinking problem, and the phenomenon of the adolescent alcoholic is no longer uncommon.

Ethyl alcohol or ethanol is the chemical depressant found in alcoholic beverages. Alcohol is created through fermentation, which is the process of converting carbohydrates into alcohol. Agricultural products commonly used in fermentation include grains, fruits, and vegetables. It has often been speculated that Stone Age Man serendipitiously discovered alcohol by imbibing the fermented liquid of fruits from a hollow tree or a warm, dank cave. The documented use of alcohol in rituals and ceremonies is many centuries old—well before the time of Christ. Both the Old and New Testaments depict a well-ingrained pattern of alcohol use in biblical culture. Alcohol was frequently employed as an elixir for a variety of medical problems during the Middle Ages. Modern society has de-emphasized the role of alcohol for medical purposes and has stressed its social value.

Alcohol has been legally available to citizens of the United States for all but thirteen years (1920–1933) of its history. Prohibition was enacted because of widespread recognition of the danger of alcohol. Prohibition was repealed because of its failure to stop the use of alcohol and the emergence of criminal control of the production and distribution of the substance.

As alcohol is absorbed into the bloodstream, the indi-

61

vidual experiences a warm and tingling sensation. The person usually experiences a temporary elevation in mood with a feeling of mild euphoria. Muscular activity, heart rate, blood pressure, and other physiological responses are not noticeably affected until the alcohol blood level approaches .05 to .10 percent. Beyond this point, individuals may show a loss of motor coordination, confusion, radical and unexplained shifts in mood, irritability, uncontrolled crying or laughing, paranoia, hostility, or suicidal thinking. The brain, kidneys, and liver are the primary victims of prolonged excessive drinking, although many other parts of the body are also adversely affected. Damage to these organs is sometimes minimized if the alcohol abuser maintains a balanced diet with plenty of protein.

Alcohol produces physiological addiction and psychological dependence. Repeated drinking creates a tolerance for alcohol, so that greater amounts of it must be ingested to produce the same effects. Alcohol addiction or alcoholism is developed over long periods (usual minimum—eighteen months) of heavy consumption. Once the addiction is evident, a few hours of abstinence may cause withdrawal effects. Delirium tremens (D.T.'s), an alcohol withdrawal syndrome, is characterized by tremor, nausea, insomnia, excessive perspiration, and elevation of blood pressure. Frightening and unusual visual and auditory hallucinations are often part of the D.T. experience. Alcohol withdrawal obviously results in extreme discomfort and may even cause death if not properly treated. Treatment usually involves the administration of Librium or Valium (minor tranquilizers). As soon as possible, a well-balanced, nutritious diet is prescribed. Subsequent to stabilizing the patient medically, he or she should be referred to Alcoholics Anonymous (A.A.), the organization most effective in treating the alcoholic. Some combination of A.A. and psychological counseling is generally recommended. Teenagers who are not alcoholics themselves but who are children of alcoholics may receive help from a national organization called Al-Ateen. This organization helps the adolescent learn to cope with the myriad problems one must face in living with an alcoholic.

In conclusion, alcohol is a dangerous drug that is subject to increasing abuse. Alcohol use is widely accepted despite its marked effect on thought, judgment, emotion, and physiology. Many people learn to use this chemical in a responsible, mature manner. These patterns are fostered, in adolescents, by adults who set an example of appropriate, temperate alcohol use. Thus, it is no surprise that alcoholics are most often born to families of alcoholics or to families who are total abstainers. Neither setting provides an example of responsible alcohol use.

Barbiturates and Tranquilizers

Barbiturates include a group of about fifty derivatives of the parent barbituric acid molecule. Barbiturates, in clinical use for the first time during the early part of the twentieth century, are most commonly used for sleep induction and sedation. They are also employed to reduce blood pressure, prevent seizure activity, and to treat various kinds of mental disorders. Mild doses of barbiturates have a calming or sedating effect; moderate doses have hypnotic effects or produce dreamless sleep; and heavier doses may produce coma or even death. These chemicals have a depressant effect on brain, heart, gastrointestinal, and particularly respiratory activity. Prolonged barbiturate use increases the dimensions and weight of the liver, reducing the efficiency of its operation. Overall, the addictive capacity of barbiturates is very similar to that of alcohol. The phenomena of tolerance and withdrawal are observed for both. However, barbiturates have an added danger—an increased likelihood of overdose. Usually, the alcohol abuser will "pass out" before he or she consumes a lethal dose, whereas a lethal dose of barbiturates may be ingested before the drug starts to take effect. Barbiturates in common use include Seconal, Nembutal, Tuinal, and Amytal. Street names include reds, yellow jackets, rainbows, and blue devils.

Methaqualone is a barbituratelike substance designed for the same medical purposes and thought to have fewer negative side effects. Quaaludes have become widely abused and have been found to possess many adverse side effects. This drug can be obtained both through prescription and on the black market. Quaaludes are created in the laboratories of pharmaceutical companies or in illicit labs primarily found in South America.

Tranquilizers are a group of substances that produce a calming effect but do not induce sleep and are not hypnotics. Tranquilizers are used to treat tension, anxiety, mental disorders, high blood pressure, and nausea. The most widely used mild tranquilizers are Valium (diazepam) and Librium (chlordiazepoxide hydrochloride), which are usually prescribed for anxiety and stress. Most studies estimate that there are over 80 million prescriptions for these drugs written each year. This involves more than 4 billion pills and adds up to over half a billion dollars in annual income to the manufacturer, Roche Laboratories. In 1973 more than 400 million dollars were spent in distributing and advertising these drugs. Although these drugs are extremely beneficial when used properly, Valium can be addictive, and Librium can produce birth defects when administered during the first thirty to fifty days of pregnancy.

Narcotics

Narcotics refer to a group of chemicals that are derived from the unripe seeds of the opium poppy or are synthetically derived to produce similar pharmacological effects. Morphine, codeine, heroin (illegal in the United States), dilhydromorphinone, meperidine (Demerol), and methadone (Dolophine) are classified as narcotics. These drugs have depressant, pain-relieving effects, tend to produce euphoria, and are extremely addictive. Common applications include relief of pain of terminal illness, postoperative pain, headache, cough, diarrhea, and treatment of narcotic addiction.

Opium and its derivatives have a long and fascinating history. Opium was used for religious purposes to produce mystic trances nearly two thousand years before the birth of Christ. Archaeologists have discovered widespread use in seventh-century A.D. Assyria. Opium trade in the Middle and Far East burgeoned in the sixteenth and seventeenth centuries. China was the first country to view opium officially as a problem and prohibited its production and use in the 1850s. England's continued sale of opium to the Chinese, despite the Emperor's law, resulted in warfare between the two countries (1842 and 1858). In 1853 the hypodermic needle was invented, and advanced scientific technology enabled morphine to be isolated from opium. Morphine was administered by injection to injured soldiers of the American Civil War, the Crimean War, and the Franco-Prussian War. Subsequently, many veterans became addicted to morphine, and this addiction came to be known as "the soldier's disease." Heroin, more potent than morphine, was introduced as a cure for morphine addiction in 1898. It was less bulky, easy to conceal, and usually administered by injection. Thus, heroin became and remained a primary abused narcotic. Hundreds of different narcotic products were legally available in America and were distributed by grocery stores, drug stores, and mail-order houses. This ended in 1914 with the Harrison Narcotic Act—a law that intended to control, not prohibit, the marketing of narcotics. Later interpretations of the law shifted toward prohibition. Even physicians who prescribed narcotics to addicts were successfully prosecuted. Governmental intervention thus became a two-edged sword—inadvertently fostering the black market in narcotics, social alienation of the user, and, worst of all, reduction of the addict to criminal status. Dr. Robert S. de Ropp, a noted biochemist, forcefully concluded:

Just why the alcoholic is tolerated as a sick man while the opiate addict is persecuted as a criminal is hard to understand. There is, in the present attitude of society in the United States toward opiate addicts, much the *same hysteria, superstition, and plain cruelty as characterized the attitude of our forefathers toward witches. Legislation reflects this cruelty and superstition. Prison sentences up to 40 years are now being imposed and the death sentence has been introduced. Perhaps one should feel thankful that the legislators have not yet reached the point of burning addicts alive. If one insists on relying on terrorism to cope with a problem which is essentially medical one may as well be logical and "go the whole hog."* *

A more humane attitude toward narcotics abusers developed during the early 1960s with the introduction of methadone maintenance programs. Methadone is a narcotic that controls heroin and morphine craving (withdrawal) and is less debilitating. A vast reduction of criminal behavior among methadone patients was observed, because stealing to purchase drugs to satisfy the craving was no longer necessary. Methadone maintenance programs have spread to most major U.S. cities and are serving thousands of addicts, including many adolescents.

Narcotics are powerful drugs that are capable of totally consuming the mind and body of the user. An emphasis on developing constructive and meaningful skills, interests, and activities without chemical intervention helps avoid the risk of narcotics addiction. However, once the habit is established, users and their families should investigate the possibility of methadone treatment while attempting to maintain family relations.

*Robert S. de Ropp, *Drugs and the Mind* (New York: St. Martin's Press, Macmillan, 1957), pp. 157–158.

Alcohol and Drugs: Use and Abuse

STIMULANTS

Stimulants are a group of chemicals that accelerate or excite the action of the central nervous system (brain and spinal cord). Naturally produced stimulants include coffee, tobacco, and cocaine. Synthetic stimulants are created through complex chemical procedures. They include amphetamines (bennies), dextroamphetamines (dexies), and methamphetamines (meth—illegal). Stimulants are medically prescribed to combat fatigue, depression, and obesity. These drugs produce euphoria; increased heart rate, blood pressure, and energy level; and loss of appetite. In some circumstances, certain stimulants are considered to be addictive; however, this is not usually the case. Once the stimulant effects wane, most individuals become irritable and depressed. Continued use of stimulants may produce a temporary psychotic state characterized by paranoia, delusions, and hallucinations.

Tobacco

Nicotine, a stimulant, is an extremely potent and destructive agent found in tobacco. Tobacco is one of the most widely abused drugs in the United States, despite continual warnings concerning the health hazards associated with its use. Approximately 40 million Americans smoke cigarettes, which is down from a figure of almost 50 million in 1966. A disturbing fact, however, is that smoking is on the increase among adolescents. Smoking is the leading cause of lung cancer, bronchitis, and emphysema. Smoking is known to contribute to cancer of the larynx, bladder, esophagus, mouth, and kidneys. Cigarette smoking leads to hardening of the arteries and many other cardiovascular problems. (Smokers are 3.5 times more likely to die of a sudden coronary than nonsmokers.) Those who are able to give up the habit before a major disease develops are able to reduce their risk of disease to that of a nonsmoker. Nicotine is a highly addictive drug that produces withdrawal symptoms. There are various treatment procedures available to aid the smoker in breaking the tobacco habit. Persons interested in these treatment procedures should contact the American Cancer Society, the American Heart Association, or a local mental health agency.

Cocaine

Cocaine use has recently become a fashionable practice among the young and affluent. Cocaine is a stimulant, usually in powder form, that is derived from the leaf of the *Erythroxylon coca*, found primarily in the Andes mountains of Peru and Bolivia. The leaf was chewed as a spiritual ritual by the Incas around A.D. 1000 and was considered a source of strength, perseverance, and fertility. Cocaine was first extracted from the plant around 1850 and was highly regarded for its medical potential. Such notables as Sigmund Freud and William Steward Halsted, one of America's most eminent surgeons and one of the four founders of Johns Hopkins Medical School, injected cocaine routinely. (Freud quit the practice after recognizing the danger of addiction, and Halsted later substituted morphine for cocaine.) In the late nineteenth and early twentieth centuries, cocaine was pervasive in American culture and was an ingredient of Coca-Cola and other soft drinks. Its use was curtailed by the Pure Food and Drug Act of 1906.

Contemporary cocaine use is widely considered chic. Cocaine is exorbitantly priced—about $2,000 per ounce for diluted cocaine. Thus, cocaine use has tremendous status appeal and carries a message. As a local newspaper put it, sniffing cocaine is like "going to Paris for breakfast." Because of its high cost, cocaine use is relatively limited among most adolescents. However, it should be noted that cocaine is increasingly more available to this group.

Synthetics

Many adolescents use synthetically produced stimulants for a variety of reasons. Doctors frequently prescribe stimulants as an aid to weight reduction, which often leads to amphetamine abuse. Moreover, synthetic stimulant drugs are frequently used for their euphoric qualities. It has been estimated that half of the amphetamines produced in legal labs wind up on the black market. Synthetic stimulants do not produce physical dependence. However, prolonged use of these drugs may result in aggressiveness, toxic reactions, compulsive behavior, paranoia, hyperactivity, and psychological dependence. Continued use of synthetic stimulants is obviously incompatible with a productive life-style because of their very high abuse potential.

HALLUCINOGENS AND MARIJUANA

Hallucinogens are a group of chemicals that produce perceptual distortions, dream images, hallucinations, and emotional exaggeration. Hallucinogens have often been referred to as psychotomimetics, dysleptics, or psychedelics. LSD, peyote (mescaline), and psilocybin (from mushrooms) are the most commonly used hallucinogens. Excluding the administration of marijuana to some glaucoma patients, possession and/or use of these drugs is illegal in the United States except in research settings.

Marijuana

As mentioned, nearly half of the adolescent population of the United States has used marijuana (also spelled *marihuana*) on at least one occasion. Marijuana has controversially been classified as a hallucinogen, although its effects are not as profound as other drugs in this category. Marijuana is a difficult substance to categorize since it contains over 250 distinct chemicals. The primary active ingredient that produces the hallucinogenic effect is THC (tetrahydrocannabinol). This chemical is found in the leaves and flower tops of the *cannabis sativa* plant that has been growing in North, Central, and South America for many centuries.

Marijuana was probably first used during religious ceremonies by the Hindus of India around 400 B.C. Its use spread to the Arab and Mediterranean areas, and by the Middle Ages, it was evident in virtually all Moslem countries. Marijuana was legally available in the United States until 1937, at which time it was declared an illegal drug by the Marihuana Tax Act. During the 1930s, many authorities attributed increases in violence and criminal behavior to the widespread use of marijuana. However, more recent studies have rejected the association between marijuana use and crime or aggression.

Marijuana smokers report a heightening of the senses and increased awareness of their environment for two to five hours after ingestion. Feelings of euphoria and personal satisfaction are often experienced, as well as unpleasant feelings of anxiety, guilt, and paranoia. Marijuana does not produce physical dependence, although psychological dependence may result. Heavy marijuana users may become lethargic and plagued with boredom. Since a significant portion of the THC collects in the gonads, marijuana has been suspected of damaging chromosomes, although this has yet to be proved. Finally, substantial evidence has been gathered to support the finding that marijuana smoking is damaging to the lungs, particularly because of the exceptionally high temperature of the smoke that is inhaled.

LSD

LSD (d-lysergic acid diethylamide) is the most potent hallucinogen, producing profound effects in the user, who usually ingests less than one millionth of an ounce. This powerful chemical was unwittingly ingested in 1943 by Albert Hofmann, a scientist for Sandoz Laboratories in Basel, Switzerland. The following is Dr. Hofmann's frequently cited report of the experience:

I had to interrupt my laboratory work in the middle of the afternoon and go home, because I was seized with a feeling of great restlessness and mild dizziness. At home, I lay down and sank into a not unpleasant delirium which was characterized by extremely excited fantasies. In a semiconscious state, with my eyes closed (I felt the daylight to be unpleasantly dazzling), fantastic visions of extraordinary realness and with a kaleidoscopic play of colors assaulted me. After about two hours this condition disappeared.*

One week later Dr. Hofmann voluntarily ingested one-quarter of a milligram of LSD (a minute amount) and reported being overwhelmed by emotion, color, and visual distortion.

LSD later became the focus of considerable attention and research concerning its medical potential. It became regarded as a possible key to the understanding and treatment of mental disorders and alcoholism. However, the drug was widely abused throughout the 1960s, which led to charges that it was a chromosome-damaging agent. (There is no preponderance of evidence on either side of this issue.) For these reasons, LSD research and psychotherapy

*Albert Hofmann, cited by John Cashman, The LSD Story (Greenwich, Conn.: Fawcett Publications, 1966), p. 31.

was largely abandoned in the United States, although these activities were continued in Europe.

The use of LSD and LSD-like drugs (peyote and psilocybin) does not constitute a pervasive problem among adolescents. First, the nature of the effect of these chemicals does not lend itself to habitual use. A very high tolerance to LSD develops, such that frequent routine administration of the drug produces little or no effect. Also, habitual drug users are apparently seeking the more consistent drug effects that are characteristic of opiates and depressants. Finally, LSD is not a toxic substance.

The most obvious danger of hallucinogens is that resulting from a loss of judgment while under their influence; for example, there are reports of individuals jumping from buildings just to experience the sensation of flight. LSD and similar hallucinogens pose considerable danger to individuals who have previous histories of mental disorder. An experience with a hallucinogen may aggravate a pre-existing mental disorder. Many users also report a flashback phenomenon that is characterized by a sudden, unexpected "psychedelic" experience days or weeks after the last "trip." This is a frightening experience for the user, particularly if it occurs in a threatening situation.

GUIDANCE

Drug abuse is a problem of increasing magnitude among contemporary adolescents. Information concerning the most widely abused drugs has been presented to promote a greater understanding of the overall problem of drug abuse. This is not a recent problem nor one that is likely to be resolved in the near future.

Several general suggestions focusing on methods of preventing drug abuse among adolescents are offered. First, parents and teenagers should remember that the seeds of drug abuse are planted during childhood. The child may observe patterns of chemical dependency, as illustrated by a parent running to the liquor cabinet or medicine chest as a means of coping with stress. The child's home may be devoid of emotional, intellectual, or spiritual fulfillment, which is readily replaced by psychotropic drugs. Poor channels of communication and tense, punitive familial relationships increase the attractiveness of drug use. Challenging activities such as art, music, and sports should be encouraged, since performance in these areas is incompatible with the use of mood-altering chemicals. Parents or other adults should not overreact upon discovering a teenager who is experimenting with drugs. Such a confrontation could rapidly escalate the intensity of underlying emotional difficulties, thereby encouraging drug abuse. Once a drug problem is suspected, consult a physician, mental health professional, or a trained pastoral counselor. These professionals are educated to help drug abusers and their families learn to cope with life's problems without the assistance of drugs. A drug-free life-style is best promoted by example, effective communication, and encouragement of constructive interests and activities.

chapter **6**

Unlawful
Behavior

Unlawful or delinquent behavior is a pervasive component of the current adolescent experience. Based on self-reports, approximately 90 percent of today's adolescents could be adjudicated as delinquent. Arrests of teenagers have nearly doubled in the past decade. Although this figure may partially reflect an increase in the ability of law enforcement agencies to identify offenders, it is generally held that more teenagers are involved in unlawful conduct than ever before. Moreover, females, affluent teenagers, rural youths, and other groups previously considered relatively free of delinquency are becoming increasingly involved in delinquent behavior. Arrests for adolescent females are increasing three times faster than for males. Currently, less than three males are arrested for every female.

The majority of offenses committed by adolescents are "property crimes" such as shoplifting, larceny, and vandalism. These are usually misdemeanors and generally are not formally adjudicated in the case of first offenders. A growing area of concern is status offenses, which include those acts that are not considered unlawful if committed by an adult. Truancy, runaway behavior, alcohol use, gambling, sexual promiscuity, and general "ungovernable behavior" are examples of status offenses. The management of adolescents who commit status offenses evokes considerable controversy, which is discussed. Less frequently observed is felonious behavior, which consists of violent crimes, thefts of large sums, or intended deployment of deadly weapons. Felonies are rarely committed by first offenders; they are usually performed by individuals with histories of misdemeanors and status offenses. Unlawful sale, possession, and ingestion of licit and illicit drugs constitute a major area of juvenile crime. The topic of drug use and its social and legal consequences has already been discussed in Chapter 5.

Most of the offenses committed by adolescents go undetected and, if discovered, are handled informally without legal intervention. Current emphasis is placed on diverting from formal court intervention those youths involved in misdemeanors and status offenses. The idea is to avoid labeling and stigmatizing these teenagers by treating them as criminals. Efforts are made to refer these people to appropriate resource agencies that provide such services as reading remediation; individual, family, and group counseling; vocational training; or family planning. Many of these young people, particularly status offenders, are found to lack adequate parental guidance and supervision and may be placed in a group-home setting. The philosophy of these programs is to supplant irresponsible, incorrigible behavior with guided constructive activity in a family-style setting that is located in the tennager's community. Meanwhile, counselors and social workers become intensely involved in assisting the young person's family in learning to manage the teenager more effectively. The adolescent returns home as soon as the environment is judged to be facilitative of normal growth and development as determined by the counselors and the youth court.

The diversion of status offenders from the legal system and from incarceration in state institutions is progressive in its greater protection of the constitutional freedoms of youths and their families. Yet many officials would agree with Judge John Peyton Collins concerning the role of the court in managing status offenders:

> Basically, I take the position that in this country we shouldn't bring people into criminal court unless they've committed a crime. But for two hundred years we have acted as though children are not people. And, for the last seventy-nine years, since we've had juvenile court, we have gotten worse and worse about what we have done to children. Now, almost eighty years after we've provided a juvenile court for them, we are still locking up kids for noncriminal offenses.*

*Excerpt from an interview printed in Change: A Juvenile Justice Quarterly, Vol. II, No. 1, 1978.

On the other hand, many people argue that status offenders in need of supervision are earmarked to become involved in serious criminal behavior and that this may be prevented through court intervention. Regardless of these disparate views, the fact remains that the vast majority of adolescents are guilty of status offenses and misdemeanors.

More serious juvenile offenses are handled through court adjudication and often through subsequent incarceration in "training" or "reform" schools, which are essentially jails for young people. Current management of youths involved in serious crimes is more punitive and less controversial than for status offenders. However, as it is for status offenders, disposition for these youths is often determined by the sex, race, and economic level of the offender, rather than by the nature of the offense.

CAUSES

There are a number of explanations and theories that attempt to explain the causes of unlawful behavior. Partial explanation lies in the fact that many of these activities generate powerful intrinsic rewards. Examples include the bored teenager who seeks thrills through driving at excessive rates of speed, often resulting in speeding tickets. Rewards for stealing include possession of the stolen item as well as peer approval. For many young people, there is also intrinsic value in drinking, sexual promiscuity, and other status offenses. A virtual plethora of incentives are available for many unlawful activities.

Scientists representing the fields of psychology, sociology, and biology have attempted to explain the etiology of delinquent and criminal behavior. Psychologists tend to emphasize the life experience and dynamics of individuals in their attempts to cope adequately with their respective environments. Sociologists adhere to broader explanations, stressing the influence of selective social factors on the behavior of the adolescent. Biologists have studied the role of genetics and biochemistry in delinquency and criminal behavior. For example, they have hypothesized that a certain genetic disorder (XYY) may be responible for the reported high rate of criminal offenses committed by afflicted individuals. This notion has yet to be proved; however, the speculation brings interesting questions to the fore.

The best explanations of the causes of unlawful behavior represent a combination of various academic disciplines. Simple, narrow perspectives do not yield valid information about such complex behavior as delinquency. Explanations of delinquency should emphasize the critical role of the peer group in its influence on the individual. A full 80 to 90 percent of adolescent offenses are committed by two or more teenagers acting together. This fact suggests that most adolescent offenders behave unlawfully in groups, whereas the same behavior would be unacceptable on an individual basis. Many teenagers completely submit to the attitudes and expectations of the peer group as a temporary substitute for parental authority.

Edwin Sutherland, a criminologist, has posed one of the most plausible theories of delinquency causation. His theory of differential association stresses the importance of learning. Criminal behavior is learned in association with individuals and groups. These associations are varied and differentiated in terms of frequency, duration, priority, and intensity. Hence, delinquency and criminal behavior are likely to result from intense, frequent associations with delinquent individuals over an extended period of time with considerable value placed on the offenders and their activities.

PREVENTION AND TREATMENT

Much of teenager involvement in unlawful behavior can be prevented. Adolescents should gradually develop frequent, enduring, and intense associations with groups involved in constructive activities. Examples include scouting, church groups, orchestras, or special-interest organizations. Adolescents should immerse themselves in academics, athletics, and the arts. Parents of teenagers should concentrate on setting better examples of responsible, law-abiding behavior. Parents who encourage older children to claim eligibility for reduced fares falsely or who use radar detection devices while speeding make a travesty of a system of values built on honesty and trust. Their children are, therefore, able to rationalize many unlawful activities.

Once a pattern of delinquent activity has been detected, it is advisable for the family to contact social and professional agencies for support. Family counseling and social services may help break the pattern of delinquent behavior if detected in the incipient stages. The adolescent who is more extensively involved in delinquent behavior may require more restrictive alternatives such as placement in a group home or training school. The idea is to remove adolescents from environments that support unlawful behavior and place them in settings that are more conducive to positive behavior change. These alternative settings may inadvertently offer even more support and training for delinquent behavior patterns. The best advice is to take action before such patterns develop!

chapter 7

Suicide

Tim is a fifteen-year-old ninth grader who was recently rushed to the emergency room of Memorial Hospital after consuming thirty to forty Valium tablets that were prescribed for his mother. Tim is overweight at 190 pounds—particularly in relation to his 5-foot, 5-inch height. Tim's alcoholic father left home about two months ago, after years of fighting, abuse, and turmoil. Both of his parents tended to discipline him through spanking, yelling, name-calling, and withdrawal of privileges. He often acted in the same manner toward his peers as his parents behaved toward him. These negative patterns served to interfere with his goal of making close friends; hence he began to withdraw into a world of TV, junk food, and malicious pranks.

Academic, social, and personal adjustment problems accelerated throughout junior high school. He became easily depressed or irritated and seemed to lose the ability to cope with minor problems. He grew more isolated socially; his mother had not observed his involvement in one close social relationship. Tim's homeroom teacher recalled that he had said "I wasn't meant to be here" on several occasions. He decided to end his struggle on a Monday afternoon while his mother was still working. He approached the medicine cabinet, as he had once before, knowing that a large bottle of five-milligram Valium tablets was stored there. This time he was committed to taking the rest of the tablets so that peace would be attained as well as to punish his parents for past transgressions. Tim's mother arrived shortly thereafter and was shocked and dismayed upon recognition of the deed. Quick and decisive action resulted in emergency medical treatment and ultimately in Tim's survival.

Unfortunately, many reports similar to the preceding fictionalized one do not end as happily. Suicide has historically been a leading cause of death among adolescents. And unfortunately the tendency toward adolescent suicide is increasing at an alarming rate. Behavioral scientists have been largely unable to explain this phenomenon or to construct theoretical models that predict suicide. This section focuses on adolescent suicide statistics, traditional explanations, and more current and useful approaches to understanding suicide.

PREVALENCE

Suicide by adolescents has increased at startling rates over the past few years. Some investigators claim a 3,000 percent increase in suicide attempts. For older adolescents, fifteen to twenty-four group, suicide is the third leading cause of death, ranking only behind accidents and homicides; whereas suicide was the fifth leading cause of death in the 1960s. Between 3,000 and 4,000 per 100,000 older adolescents attempt suicide in the United States each year. Approximately 10 attempts per 100,000 end in death.

Suicide knows no social boundaries. For successful suicides, males outnumber females by 3 to 1, whereas for suicide attempters, females outnumber males approximately 2.5 to 1. Only slightly higher suicide rates are found in nonwhite populations, which usually report greater alcoholism, unemployment, educational deficiency, and disintegration of cultural, familial, and spiritual solidarity as compared to whites.

In terms of methods of suicide, males tend to choose firearms and explosives. Females prefer poison in the form of toxic dosages of prescription drugs or carbon monoxide poisoning. Hanging and suffocation are methods of suicide employed by both groups.

PROBLEMS IN INVESTIGATION

It should be noted that for several reasons, suicide is an extremely difficult subject to investigate objectively. First, many suicides and suicide attempts go unreported, primarily because of the stigma associated with suicide. Reports of suicide attempts vary according to race, income, religious affiliation, sex, education, age, and other socio-economic factors. Also, it is difficult in the study of successful suicides to obtain information about the victim's personality and general psychological profile. (Obviously, data are available only when evaluations were performed prior to the act.) Thus, most behavioral scientists study individuals who attempt suicide and then apply the data to cases of successful suicide. Although there may be different variables and processes at work, the study of suicide attempters is generally thought to be useful in making inferences to successful suicides. Keep in mind that the overall purpose of the study of suicide is to predict scientifically and thus prevent suicide.

CAUSES: COMPLEX AND ELUSIVE

Numerous causes of suicide have been suggested by professionals in several academic disciplines. Various social and psychological factors have been most often cited as causes of suicide. More recently, physiological factors such as adrenal steroids, organic brain damage as indexed by abnormal EEGs, extreme dysmenorrhea, and pregnancy have been implicated as causal elements. Only one thing is certain—the cause of suicide lies in a complex interaction of variables that will not be readily discovered or explained.

The first modern attempts to explain the phenomenon of suicide were made by scholars of psychological theory. The personality of the individual as determined by experiences in early childhood predisposed the individual to the act of suicide. Freudian theorists maintained that each individual possesses a life force (libido) and a death force (mortido, as it was later called). Mortido is observed in such acts as smoking or driving without seat belts; and in cases of a more forceful mortido, suicide results.

Emile Durkheim, a renowned sociologist, grew frustrated with the inability of Freudian and other psychological theorists to predict and explain suicide. Durkheim rejected psychological theory and looked toward social antecedents of suicide for more useful information. Durkheim asserted that suicide is a result of social disorganization as reflected in the dissipation of culture, an increase in alcoholism and unemployment, the breakdown of the family unit, and other social variables. Although Durkheim, like Freud, was a great scientist and scholar, his theories and observations did not enhance the predictability of suicide.

Dr. Jerry Jacob, a contemporary sociologist, indicated that Durkheim's greatest fallacy was the total rejection of the importance of the individual's psychological makeup. Dr. Jacob has proposed a new and more useful framework for understanding and predicting suicide based on a combination of social and psychological theory. Dr. Jacob sees suicide as a progressive phenomenon that 80 percent of adolescent attempters experience. First, most suicide attempters have a history of personal and adjustment problems that escalate shortly before the occurrence of the act. The person is progressively unable to cope with ordinary life stress. The individual also becomes progressively socially withdrawn, and meaningful social relationships dissolve. Finally, the attempter develops a rationale or conceptual justification for the act (e.g., "I am of no use to anyone" or "there is no reason for me to live"). Interestingly, people who attempt suicide initially exhibit less extreme forms of maladjustment, which usually progress from simple rebelliousness to withdrawing to running away from home and finally to attempted suicide.

WHAT SHOULD YOU DO?

Dr. Jacob and other scholars have presented promising approaches to the understanding and prevention of suicide. It is important to educate the public in recognizing and acting on these common denominators or progressive steps of suicide. Once it has been decided that a person may be suicidal, one should first ask about any plans or intentions of self-destruction. Many people give ample warning and will actually state exactly what they plan to do. Second, you should encourage the person to seek qualified professional help. Mental health professionals are extensively trained to handle the suicidal individual effectively. They offer support, medication, self-exploration, consideration of alternatives, and other methods of help. Third, one should be supportive of the individual in such a way that feelings of self-worth are maximized and feelings of rejection are minimized. Readily acknowledge the individual's strengths, and attempt to bring this person into contact with others who will be supportive.

Suicide is an ever-increasing threat to the well-being of

adolescents. Suicide occurs in all segments of our society. The understanding and prediction of suicide are elusive endeavors, although some progress has been made toward these ends. Early recognition of the common variables coupled with professional treatment may help to reverse the rising incidence of adolescent suicide.

chapter 8

Psychological Disorders

The following referrals might be made to a community mental health center.

NAME: *Bill G.*   AGE: *17*
REFERRAL SOURCE: *Principal, Hamilton High School*
PRESENTING PROBLEM: *Loss of interest in school. Drop in grades from B+ to failing. Excessive absences.*

NAME: *Norma N.*   AGE: *14*
REFERRAL SOURCE: *Youth Court*
PRESENTING PROBLEM: *Hostile and aggressive behavior. Truancy. Frequent fighting. Shoplifting. Foster parents unable to control her behavior.*

NAME: *Alice P.*   AGE: *18*
REFERRAL SOURCE: *Family doctor.*
PRESENTING PROBLEM: *"Seizurelike" episodes with no known organic cause. Indifference to symptoms. Presently hospitalized for further evaluation.*

NAME: *Barry T.*   AGE: *16*
REFERRAL SOURCE: *Parents*
PRESENTING PROBLEM: *Severe agitation and uncontrollable behavior. Talks to self and hears voices. Thinks family is trying to poison his food. Refuses to eat or drink with family.*

NAME: *Sue B.*   AGE: *14*
REFERRAL SOURCE: *Parents*
PRESENTING PROBLEM: *Weight loss of thirty pounds over last three months. Decrease in food intake over past*

three months. Eats very little. Reports no appetite. No physical cause found for weight loss.

The foregoing individuals are experiencing a few of the many psychological disorders observed during adolescence. Approximately 10 percent of adolescents experience psychological problems severe enough to require professional help.

The causes of psychological problems in adolescence are varied and not completely understood in all cases. In most instances, problems result from an interaction of several different factors. Childhood experiences, personality, socioeconomic factors, family structure, current environmental stress, and possibly genetic influences contribute to psychological disorders. The importance of each factor varies with the individual and the nature of the problem.

Problems vary in severity, period of onset, and duration. Some problems show rapid onset, whereas others surface slowly over a number of years. Some represent the continuation of childhood disorders, and others have their origins in adolescence. Some result from a specific identifiable stress, and others result from less identifiable factors.

The adolescent alone may be able to solve relatively minor problems, although in some instances, the help of peers, parents, or other significant persons may be necessary. More serious problems may require professional intervention in the form of short-term counseling and/or family therapy. Severe disturbances may require intensive therapy, hospitalization, or the use of medication.

Treatment procedures (the topic of Chapter 9) vary and should be designed on an individual basis. The best treatment procedures are tailored to the specific requirements and circumstances of the adolescent. As practicing clinicians, we know all too well that what works for one adolescent may not work for another.

A case-by-case description of various problems observed during adolescence follows. The cases themselves are fictitious (in order to preserve confidentiality), but they present composites of the hundreds of adolescents we have treated over the years. They represent a sampling of adolescents commonly treated by community mental health centers, family service clinics, and private practitioners.

TRANSIENT SITUATIONAL DISTURBANCE, ADJUSTMENT REACTION OF ADOLESCENCE

Bill G.'s social worker recorded the following information during Bill's first visit to the mental health center.

SOCIAL HISTORY

BEHAVIORAL OBSERVATIONS:

Bill G. is a handsome, seventeen-year-old male. He was neatly groomed and casually dressed. He was rather anxious at the beginning of the interview and was initially reluctant to discuss his problems. He gradually became more relaxed and was able to "open up" toward the end of the session. Bill is intelligent, articulate, and shows some insight into his difficulties. He appears willing to receive help.

Bill was referred by his high school principal, Mr. Jordan. Over the last nine weeks, Bill's grades have dropped from B+ to failing. He has been absent from school on the average of one to two days per week. Bill states that he cannot concentrate on his studies and misses school whenever he has not prepared his assignments. Bill reports sleeping problems, worry, and periodic feelings of depression. He has decreased his outside activities and does not see his friends as frequently as he used to. Bill reports problems in getting along with his stepfather. He portrays his stepfather as being overly restrictive and punitive. Bill states that his problems started approximately four months ago.

FAMILY AND PERSONAL HISTORY:

Bill comes from an upper-middle-class home. He lives with his mother, stepfather, and fifteen-year-old sister. His parents divorced when he was four years old, and his mother remarried six months ago. Bill visits his natural father for one month each summer.

Bill's mother is employed as a real estate agent, and his stepfather is an assistant manager at a local automobile dealership.

Bill's developmental history is normal. He displayed no serious adjustment problems prior to the current mental health contact. Bill indicates that he was not enthusiastic about his mother's remarriage, but no major conflicts arose during his mother's courtship.

Problems began after the marriage, when the stepfather began assuming more responsibility for making family decisions and disciplining Bill and his younger sister. This led to conflicts between Bill's mother and stepfather. Relationships at home have been strained over the past two or three months.

This is the stepfather's first marriage. He has had little experience with teenagers.

MENTAL AND HEALTH HISTORY:

This is Bill's first mental health contact. He reports no present physical ailments. He had the usual childhood diseases. He broke his arm playing football at age twelve and was hospitalized for three days.

SOCIAL BEHAVIOR:

Bill has several close male friends. He dates occasionally and has no steady girl friend. His social contacts have decreased over the past few months.

VOCATIONAL AND EDUCATIONAL HISTORY:

Bill is in the twelfth grade at Hamilton High School. He is in a precollege program and plans to enter State University next fall. Prior to the last nine weeks, he has always been an average to above-average student.

He has a newspaper route and has worked at various summer jobs.

Bill denies regular drug use. He admits to trying marijuana on two occasions. He drinks an occasional beer with his friends.

IMPRESSIONS:

Bill appears to be experiencing adjustment difficulties because of the change in his family situation. He resents his stepfather's intrusion into the family and the new restrictions that have been placed on him. Communication appears to be poor between Bill and his stepfather. This has led to conflicts involving all family members. Bill has experienced a loss of status within the family unit, since he is no longer the senior male family member.

Bill has maintained a good relationship with his mother. However, since her remarriage, she spends less time with Bill and his sister.

PROVISIONAL DIAGNOSIS:

Transient situational disturbance, adjustment reaction of adolescence.

RECOMMENDATIONS:

1. Bill should be referred for short-term individual counseling. Specific goals are for Bill (a) to gain insight into his current problems and (b) to develop methods for properly dealing with them.

2. The entire family should be referred for family counseling. Specific counseling goals for the family are (a) to gain insight into the current family difficulties, (b) to improve lines of communication, and (c) to develop strategies for improving the family's adjustment to the recent changes.
3. Bill's mother and stepfather should be referred to an adolescent parents' group in order (a) to gain information concerning adolescent behavior and (b) to learn about behavior management techniques as applied to adolescents.
4. The school authorities should be consulted about (a) Bill's school progress and (b) how missed work can be made up.

Transient situational disturbances encompass some of the more common adolescent psychological disorders and are caused by situational (environmental) stress. This diagnostic category is based on clinical data indicating that once the stress is identified and removed, the adolescent will return to normal psychological functioning. The onset of the disorder is typically sudden and coincides with the onset of the precipitating stress. The severity of the adolescent's *adjustment reaction* varies and correlates, to some extent, with the intensity of the stress. Behavioral manifestations of adjustment reactions range from anxiety, depression, withdrawal, and hostile behavior to confusion and temporary but generalized personality disorganization. Episodes of disturbed behavior are typically short-lived. Short-term individual counseling, group therapy, and family counseling are common methods of treatment.

Bill's case represents one way in which an adjustment reaction can develop. Other common causes are failure at some life experience (e.g., failure to gain admission to a preferred college), a traumatic personal experience (e.g., temporary disability following an accident), conflict with peers (e.g., rejection by peers), and problems with the opposite sex (e.g., breakup of a male–female relationship).

BEHAVIOR DISORDER, UNSOCIALIZED AGGRESSIVE REACTION OF ADOLESCENCE

Norma N. was referred to the mental health center by the Youth Court for psychological evaluation. The psychologist filed the following report.

CONFIDENTIAL PSYCHOLOGICAL EVALUATION OF NORMA N.

REASON FOR EVALUATION:

Norma N., a fourteen-year-old female, was referred for evaluation by the Youth Court. Norma was recently charged with shoplifting. She has been before the Youth Court on several occasions and has a history of fighting at school, striking a teacher on one occasion, and truancy. We have been requested to provide information about intellectual and personality functioning.

BACKGROUND INFORMATION:

Background information was supplied by a County Youth Court Worker. Norma was placed in foster care at age seven. She and her two siblings were abandoned by their mother and placed in foster care by the County Department of Human Services. The mother's whereabouts are unknown. Norma has displayed behavioral problems since being placed in foster care, and she has been in five foster homes over the last seven years.

Norma is failing the seventh grade at Hillcrest Junior High School. She was retained in the fourth grade but has been socially promoted ever since. Her teachers and foster parents describe her as uncooperative, belligerent, and aggressive. Norma relates poorly to her peers and has few friends. It is reported that she has been sexually involved with several older teenage boys.

This is Norma's fourth mental health contact.

BEHAVIORAL OBSERVATIONS:

Norma is tall and well developed for her age. She was casually dressed in a sweat shirt and blue jeans. She was generally uncooperative, stating that she did not need to see a "head doctor." Her motivation to do well on the tests presented to her was minimal. She appeared to delight in discussing her various exploits, especially those involving sexual relations with older males.

TEST RESULTS:

Norma scored within the low-average range of general intelligence. Her lack of motivation probably depressed her score, and with improved motivation, she should be able to score within the average range. Testing indicated relative strengths within the nonverbal and visual-motor areas. She displays a relative weakness in abstract reasoning, general information, and knowledge of appropriate behavior within social and interpersonal situations.

Norma's academic achievement skills are on a fifth-grade level. This is below her current grade placement and probably reflects her poor school attendance and lack of academic motivation.

Personality evaluation reveals feelings of low self-esteem, isolation, loneliness, and poor impulse control. Norma is reluctant to form close personal relationships and shows a basic distrust of others. Her hostile and aggressive behavior is most likely a reaction to strong feelings of rejection. Her anger toward those around her is sometimes expressed by antisocial activities.

Norma has failed to develop the requisite social skills and self-control to enable her to deal effectively with her environment.

DIAGNOSTIC IMPRESSION:

Behavior disorder of adolescence, unsocialized aggressive reaction.

RECOMMENDATIONS:

1. Norma should be referred for individual therapy with the aim of (a) building self-confidence, (b) teaching her to deal with anger and frustration in socially appropri-

ate ways, and (c) teaching appropriate social skills within a one-to-one situation through modeling and role-play techniques.

2. She should be enrolled in adolescent group therapy with the aim of (a) teaching her appropriate social skills within a group situation and (b) teaching her how to interact with her peers.

3. Consultation should be provided to Norma's school counselor regarding her academic difficulties. (An individualized instructional program should be devised to meet Norma's academic needs.)

4. Norma's foster parents should be enrolled in the parent effectiveness group. The aim is to teach them how to deal better with Norma's behavioral difficulties.

Other frequently occurring behavior disorders of adolescence include withdrawing reaction, overanxious reaction, runaway reaction, and group delinquent reaction. Although some overlap exists, each disorder has quite identifiable symptoms and characteristics. In reality, adolescents usually show mixed symptoms and behaviors.

Behavior disorders are usually more serious than the previously discussed adjustment reactions and typically develop over a longer period of time. They are also more resistant to treatment.

Adolescents with behavior disorders usually display disturbed interpersonal relationships and inadequate social skills. Common characteristics are immaturity, lack of self-confidence, anxiety, timidity, overdependence, feelings of rejection, and socially inappropriate behavior. It is important to recognize that such adolescents have serious psychological problems. The problems are usually long-term and may develop into more severe adult disorders. Intensive professional treatment is usually required.

HYSTERICAL NEUROSIS, CONVERSION TYPE

Alice P., an eighteen-year-old female, was referred to the mental health center for psychiatric consultation by her family physician. Alice had experienced three "seizurelike" episodes over the past four days. During each episode she fell to the floor and lost "consciousness" for approximately fifteen minutes. Each episode occurred at home. Alice was not injured physically from the falls, and her family physician could find no physical cause for her disorder. Alice was referred to the mental health center's staff psychiatrist for consultation. The psychiatric report reads as follows:

MENTAL HEALTH CONSULTATION

PATIENT: *Alice P.*   ADMITTING PHYSICIAN: *Dr. V.*

CONSULTANT: *Dr. M., Staff Psychiatrist*

The patient is an attractive eighteen-year-old female with no previous mental health contact. She was alert and reasonably cooperative. She reports no physical complaints. The case record indicates the occurrence of three "seizurelike" episodes over a four-day period. Results of neurological and physical examinations are negative.

Mental status evaluation reveals a talkative, somewhat detached, and mildly anxious adolescent. She shows no overt symptoms of depression. She was well oriented with respect to time, place, and person. Her thoughts were logical and coherent. She shows no evidence of delusions, ideas of reference, or paranoid ideation. She denies experiencing auditory or visual hallucinations: She displays no evidence of psychosis.

Intellectual resources are intact. She appears to be average to above average intellectually.

The patient avoids discussing her presenting symptoms. She acts as if the episodes have never occurred. When confronted with her symptoms, she appears unconcerned and frequently asks when she will be released from the hospital.

The parents indicate that Alice tends to show mood swings (emotional lability) and frequently overreacts to stressful situations. The parents feel that although Alice is intelligent and well behaved, she is immature, self-conscious, and overdependent on them. Alice graduated from high school last month and has only recently agreed to attend an out-of-town college. She wanted to attend a nearby junior college but finally agreed to attend her mother's alma mater after considerable pressure from her. The parents felt that it would do Alice good to be away from home and on her own for a while.

DIAGNOSTIC IMPRESSION:

Hysterical neurosis, conversion type.

RECOMMENDATIONS:

1. *Relaxation therapy to reduce anxiety*
2. *Individual psychotherapy*
3. *Family counseling*

Alice's case is an example of a hysterical neurosis, conversion type. Anxiety forms the basis of this disorder. In psychological terms, the anxiety is manifested (converted) into physical symptoms for which there is no organic (physiological) basis. The physical symptoms typically serve a useful psychological purpose by enabling the individual to avoid an anxiety-producing situation or task. Alice's "seizures" would prevent her from having to go away to college. An interesting aspect of this disorder is the adolescent's casual attitude toward the symptoms. It should be noted that although the symptoms have no organic basis, the adolescent is not faking them (malingering). The adolescent actually "experiences" the symptoms as if there were a physical cause.

The psychiatric report indicates that Alice was emotionally labile and immature. She had a history of overreacting to stress. Her personality makeup may have influenced her to deal with anxiety in a "hysterical" manner.

Other neurotic conditions experienced by adolescents include anxiety neurosis, phobic neurosis, and depressive neurosis. These disorders have certain distinguishing characteristics, but the common element underlying each is the experience of anxiety. Anxiety is subjectively experienced as dread, apprehension, or fear. With regard to anxiety neurosis, anxiety is generalized and not restricted to specific situations. The opposite is true in phobic neurosis, where anxiety is associated with a specific object or situation (e.g., speaking before large groups or taking tests). Depressive neurosis is distinguished by an excessive reaction to a specific event (e.g., loss of a loved one) or to an internal conflict.

Treatment usually involves counseling or psychotherapy, relaxation therapy (training in methods to reduce anxiety), and family counseling. Medication is occasionally used as an adjunct to treatment to help reduce anxiety.

SCHIZOPHRENIA, PARANOID TYPE

Barry T., age sixteen, was brought to the mental health center's crisis unit by his parents. The parents told the psychologist on duty that Barry had been acting strangely for about two weeks. He had become withdrawn and stayed in his room most of the time. Although it was summer, Barry refused to open his window and had even taped it shut. He could be heard at night talking to himself. For the last two days, Barry has refused to eat with the family. He has eaten only canned foods that he prepared himself. When questioned about this last night, Barry became argumentative and accused his family of trying to poison him. He became extremely agitated and threw a lamp at his father. Barry had to be restrained by his father and older brothers.

The psychologist interviewed Barry and immediately referred him to the center's inpatient unit. His report states:

CRISIS CONTACT SUMMARY

NAME: *Barry T.*   AGE: *16*

REFERRED BY: *Mr. and Mrs. John T. (parents)*

APPEARANCE: *Tall, thin male (6 ft./145 lbs.), sloppy appearance, long uncombed hair, unshaven, wearing soiled T-shirt, jogging shoes, and shorts.*

BEHAVIOR DURING INTERVIEW: *Erratic, fluctuating from hostility to indifference and passiveness, laughed and smiled inappropriately, stared off into space, easily distracted, rapid speech.*

MOOD: *Emotionally labile, mood swings, guarded, apprehensive.*

THOUGHTS: *Disorganized and vague. States he is being plotted against, family trying to poison him, forces are trying to take over his mind, and he can hear voices plotting against him. Paranoid delusions, has developed a new theory of electricity.*

INTELLECT: *Disturbed reasoning, memory, and judgment. Disoriented with respect to day, date, and year. States year is 1872.*

ALCOHOL AND DRUG USE: *Denied—substantiated by family.*

PREVIOUS MENTAL HEALTH CONTACT: *Seen for evaluation at age thirteen because of adjustment problems in school.*

RECOMMENDATIONS: *Refer to inpatient unit for further evaluation and treatment.*

PROVISIONAL DIAGNOSIS: *Presently psychotic, consider schizophrenia, paranoid type.*

Barry's case represents a severe type of psychological disorder that falls under the general category of psychosis. In the psychoses, reality contact is significantly impaired, and the adolescent's behavior is typically disorganized and bizarre. The disorder may affect the adolescent's emotional life (affective psychosis), thoughts (schizophrenia), or a combination of both. The adolescent's ability to meet the ordinary demands of life is significantly impaired, and behavior is grossly disturbed.

Barry is experiencing a subcategory of psychosis, termed *schizophrenia, paranoid type.* In this disorder, the adolescent typically shows delusions of persecution (i.e., thoughts of being plotted against) and grandeur (i.e., thoughts of being very important, famous, or extremely wealthy). Auditory and/or visual hallucinations are common, as is bizarre and hostile behavior.

Although psychosis is a rare disorder (occurring at a rate of approximately 1 percent in the general population), it is one of the primary causes of psychiatric hospitalization for adolescents. It is a severe disorder that affects the total functioning of the individual. In acute forms, the adolescent invariably requires intensive long-term psychiatric and psychological treatment. However, the disorder can be controlled, and the adolescent can be rehabilitated to relatively normal functioning.

The causes of psychoses are varied and not completely

understood. Some specific forms result from brain injury due to physical trauma or drug effects. Other forms are probably due to environmental factors, psychological stress, biochemical and genetic factors.

ANOREXIA NERVOSA

Sue B. was referred to the mental health center's intermediate care unit by her family doctor. The intake worker obtained the following information from Sue and her parents.

INTAKE SUMMARY

Sue B., a fourteen-year-old female, is being transferred to this unit from Memorial Hospital by Dr. Benton S. Sue was hospitalized one week ago for medical evaluation following a weight loss of thirty pounds over the past three months. Dr. S. found no medical cause for the weight loss and drastic reduction in Sue's appetite. Dr. S. made a diagnosis of anorexia nervosa and is referring Sue here for psychological evaluation and behavior therapy.

Sue comes from a middle-class home and lives with her parents and two sisters (ages nineteen and twelve). The parents indicate that Sue had been well adjusted as a child and has always been a good student.

Sue was overweight until age twelve, when she started to become interested in boys. She went on a diet pre-

scribed by her physician and lost twenty-five pounds over a six-month period. Since that time, Sue has been overly conscious about her weight and dieted every time she gained a pound or two. Her weight in relation to her height has been decreasing over the past two years.

Two months ago Sue's appetite decreased dramatically, and she began to experience rapid weight loss. Attempts by her parents and physician to reason with her and encourage her to resume normal eating have failed. Prior to hospitalization at Memorial Hospital, Sue had not eaten in three days. She will drink small amounts of water.

Sue is 5 feet, 4 inches tall and weighs 87 pounds.

Sue is experiencing a disorder called anorexia nervosa (compulsive avoidance of food accompanied by loss of appetite and rapid weight loss). This disorder, though relatively rare in the general population, is experienced by a disproportionately high number of young (adolescent and early adult) middle- and upper-class females. Although the causes of this disorder are not completely understood, many adolescents who develop anorexia nervosa have background histories similar to Sue's. Frequently, there is a history of childhood and early adolescent obesity followed by a diet that initially produces reasonable weight loss. Typically, an overconcern about weight develops, and the adolescent attempts to avoid weight gain at any cost. There may be a history of ridicule by family and peers, and praise and encouragement are offered following initial weight loss. Some of these adolescents have been described as shy, timid, naive, and overcontrolled. The cessation of eating in acute forms of *anorexia nervosa* is typically accompanied by attention from family members. Some experts believe that the attention provides a "secondary gain" for the adolescent by enabling her to control the family and possibly to express anger and hostility toward the family covertly.

Successful treatment approaches employ a combination of behavior therapy and counseling. An attempt is made to reverse the adolescent's eating patterns by systematically rewarding approaches to food and eating and withdrawing attention and other rewards for noneating. Inpatient treatment is usually prescribed, since rewards (e.g., social contact, TV viewing, opportunity to engage in preferred activities) can be controlled and administered as reinforcers for eating. Counseling focuses on other problems that may have contributed to the adolescent's decrease in eating.

The psychological disorders discussed in this chapter represent a sampling of the many types of problems experienced by adolescents. We have made no attempt to include all disorders. Such a task is beyond the scope of this book. Rather, we have attempted to highlight disorders that are frequently seen by mental health professionals and others who work with adolescents. Our goal is to familiarize the reader with the range of problems experienced by adolescents and the various causes of such problems.

The vast majority of individuals never experience such significant emotional conflicts during adolescence. When problems do arise, most of them are of the transient situational nature and can be resolved without professional help.

In a small number of cases, similar to those discussed in this chapter, professional help is required.

It is important for those who come in contact with adolescents to be sensitive to situations where professional help is required and to guide the adolescent accordingly. Sudden changes in behavior, withdrawal, depression, excessive anxiety, a drop in school performance, and hostile and aggressive behavior should all be investigated as signs of emotional disorder. Prompt professional consultation can usually help alleviate most adolescent problems and prevent them from becoming more serious.

chapter **9**

Getting Help

In the previous chapter we discussed a number of psychological disorders experienced by adolescents. We attempted to illustrate the various symptoms and causes of adolescent emotional problems. Our discussion was not all-inclusive, nor was it meant to enable the reader to diagnose emotional problems without professional consultation. Rather, our goal was to familiarize the reader with adolescent disorders and to create an awareness of situations in which professional help is needed.

The present chapter focuses on where to get help, the types of help available, what individuals provide services for troubled adolescents, and treatment methods. No single profession, group of individuals, or agency has a monopoly on adolescent counseling. Accepted treatment procedures are as diverse as the problems adolescents experience. Each profession, agency, and treatment procedure has something to offer.

Troubled adolescents become involved in treatment in various ways. Much depends on the type of problem experienced, the manner in which symptoms are manifested, and available community services.

THE HELPING PROFESSIONS

Teachers and Guidance Counselors

Many problems experienced by adolescents are initially observed in the school environment. Such problems may take the form of a drop in grades, loss of motivation, excessive absences, social withdrawal, or troublesome behavior. The classroom teacher, who is usually the first to notice such changes, may help in many ways. Through training and experience, most teachers are aware of the problems adolescents encounter. Depending on the problem, the adolescent may be more willing to confide in a favorite teacher (and to accept his or her suggestions) than to confide in his or her parents. Teachers may also provide valuable information to parents about the nature of a problem and how it is being manifested. In smaller school systems, teachers know students quite well and are attuned to changes in behavior. Hence, these teachers are a good resource for solving problems or referring the adolescent to an appropriate helping person or agency.

Many schools employ guidance counselors (or school psychologists) to work with adolescents having problems. The experience and training of counselors vary; however, most hold an academic degree (a master's or doctorate) in counseling or school psychology. The school counselor is typically skilled in recognizing adolescent emotional, behavioral, and academic problems and in developing programs to deal with such problems. The counselor may work with the adolescent on an individual basis or coordinate a treatment program with the adolescent's teachers. Parents may also be asked to participate in the program established for the adolescent. The school counselor provides an excellent initial resource for parents of troubled adolescents. Counselors are typically knowledgeable about other community resources that may be of help.

Parents who suspect problems are advised to consult with school authorities initially. Many problems can be handled at this level. If more specialized services are required, school authorities are usually able to refer adolescents and parents to effective treatment agencies.

Family Physicians

Family physicians provide another initial resource for the identification of adolescent problems. Physicians' interest and training in dealing with emotional disorders vary, and much depends on the family's relationship with the particular doctor. Although most physicians are too busy to provide long-term counseling, they may be able to rule out physical causes for the adolescent's difficulty. The physician is typically aware of the family situation and may provide valuable insight into the adolescent's problem. Physicians are usually aware of community mental health resources available to the adolescent and family.

Clergy

Families frequently turn to their minister, priest, or rabbi in time of need. Many members of the clergy have training and experience in various aspects of counseling and psychology. Some have obtained advanced degrees in one of these areas in addition to their religious training. Members of the clergy are sensitive to the needs of the family and may be quite familiar with the particular problem situation. Depending on the family's religious convictions and the part religion plays in the lives of its members, clergy may prove to be a valuable resource. Members of the clergy are frequently able to provide short-term individual and family counseling. In addition, they may provide emotional support for the family during a crisis and help prevent more serious problems. In small rural communities, the minister, priest, or rabbi may be the only individual possessing the skills, interest, and training to help the adolescent. Although they often differ in their ideas of the causes and handling of emotional disorders, most clergy are familiar with community resources and are willing to help the family locate needed services.

Psychiatrists, Psychologists, and Social Workers

Psychiatry, psychology, and social work are typically thought of as the core mental health professions. Although the training and specific skills of individuals in each profession differ, there is a large amount of overlap.

The psychiatrist is a physician (medical doctor) with specialized training in the treatment of mental and emotional disorders. The psychiatrist attends a medical school and usually does a residency in a psychiatric hospital or psychiatric training facility. The psychiatrist is a specialist in the medical aspects of emotional disorders. Psychiatrists are skilled in counseling and psychotherapy. They can prescribe medications for the alleviation of symptoms of emotional illness.

Most psychologists hold a Ph.D. degree and are usually trained in university graduate schools. The psychologist's study emphasizes various aspects of normal and abnormal behavior, human development, counseling, and psychotherapy. The psychologist receives specialized training in diagnostic psychological testing (i.e., intelligence testing, personality evaluation). In addition to graduate training, most psychologists intern at a specialized training facility or have other supervised experience before they are allowed to practice independently. Psychologists do not prescribe medications.

Social workers typically have a master's of social work degree (MSW) that usually requires a two-year course of graduate study following college. Two additional years of supervised experience are required for certification by the

Academy of Certified Social Workers. A doctorate degree in social work is offered at some schools, and an increasing number of people are trained at this level.

Psychiatrists, psychologists, and social workers are primary care givers. They may work as private practitioners or may be employed by public agencies, hospitals, institutions, schools, colleges, or universities.

COMMUNITY RESOURCES

Communities differ in the types of services they provide for those with psychological problems. Larger communities typically have many resources. Resources in smaller rural communities may be limited. Locating qualified professional help may be difficult in some areas, but knowing where to look can ease the process.

Community Mental Health Centers

Community mental health centers serve most of the nation. Each center serves a specific area (catchment area), which may range from a section of a city, in large urban areas, to several counties in rural areas. Some offer services in a single centralized location, and others are decentralized and offer services at several locations (satellite clinics). Some centers are autonomous, free-standing agencies, whereas others are associated with hospitals or other social service agencies. Centers differ greatly in size, level of development, and services and programs offered. Most offer certain basic programs that include inpatient services for individuals with serious psychological problems requiring short-term hospital care, outpatient services (usually the most frequently used service), twenty-four-hour emergency (crisis) service, partial (day) hospitalization, consultation and education services, children's services, services for the elderly, aftercare and transitional services for people released from state hospitals, and alcohol and drug-abuse services. Services for adolescents may be included with some of the preceding programs (e.g., inpatient, outpatient, drug and alcohol, children's) or may be part of more specialized programs (e.g., Youth Court services, adolescent halfway houses). Centers are staffed by individuals representing a number of specialties. Centers typically employ psychiatrists, psychologists, social workers, counselors, alcohol and drug-abuse specialists, nurses, and other mental health professionals. Centers are usually publicly funded (by a combination of local, state, and federal funds), and fees are based on the family's ability to pay.

Many centers use a team approach to treatment and are able to provide a number of coordinated services to the adolescent and family. This can be a great advantage in dealing with complex problems where the services of more than one professional are needed. For example, the adolescent and family may be seen by several staff members making up the treatment team. The psychologist may provide diagnostic and individual counseling services. The psychiatrist may prescribe medication and supervise inpatient care if needed. Social workers may provide group and family therapy or liaison services with other agencies. Centers work closely with other community agencies and are able to coordinate services with them. Consultation services may be provided to the school so that officials will be advised of the adolescent's academic needs. Community mental health centers usually have their phone numbers listed in the Yellow Pages under "Mental Health," "Family Counseling," "Marriage and Family Counselors," "Psychologists," "Social Workers," and "Suicide Prevention."

Family and Children's Service Programs

Some communities have family and children's services programs (clinics, centers). These programs may be associated with mental health centers, or they may be autonomous. Services offered by such programs vary, and many of them may be similar to those offered by community mental health centers.

College and University Counseling Centers and Psychology Clinics

Most larger colleges and universities maintain counseling centers that offer mental health services for enrolled students. Counseling centers are usually staffed by mental health professionals (e.g., psychologists, social workers, and counselors) and supervised student trainees.

Universities and medical schools may also offer mental health services to the general public. Services are usually provided by supervised graduate students, interns, and residents specializing in mental-health-related areas.

Crisis Lines and
Information and Referral Services

Some communities maintain crisis lines and/or information and referral services. Crisis lines (often associated with community mental health centers) provide telephone emergency services. Manned by trained volunteers and/or mental health professionals, crisis lines provide counseling over the telephone and information on where to obtain further help. Crisis lines are particularly valuable during nonbusiness hours (evenings, weekends, and holidays), when other services are typically unavailable.

A few communities maintain information and referral services. Such services may be contacted by phone and will provide information on where to get help for a particular problem.

TREATMENT PROCEDURES

Individual Counseling and Psychotherapy

Individual counseling and psychotherapy are the most frequently used mode of treatment for adolescents. The adolescent meets with a counselor or therapist on a one-to-one basis. Various treatment strategies exist, and the counseling approach depends largely on the philosophical orientation of the treatment professional (beliefs regarding the nature, causes, and methods of dealing with emotional disorders) and on the nature of the adolescent's problem. Individual treatment appraoches vary from traditional psychoanalysis (based on the writings of Sigmund Freud and others) to behavioral approaches (based on learning theory and principles derived from experimental psychology). Each approach has its advocates and its critics.

Our preference is for a goal-oriented problem-solving approach. This approach calls for an assessment of the adolescent's present situation, an attempt to identify those factors that are contributing to the adolescent's current problems, and the development of problem-solving strategies. For example, an adolescent with problems in making friends and interacting with peers might be found to be deficient in social skills. Such an adolescent might also experience anxiety in interpersonal situations. Treatment would involve an assessment of present social skills with an attempt to identify strengths and weaknesses. Treatment would also involve instruction in methods to capitalize on strengths and improve deficient skills. The adolescent would be trained in methods of reducing anxiety in interpersonal situations. The goal would be to improve the adolescent's interpersonal relationships and reduce his or her anxiety in the company of others.

Other adolescent problems would require different treatment strategies; however, the basic principles remain the same. They are (1) assessment of the adolescent's current problem, (2) identification of factors contributing to the problem, (3) the development of specific strategies to remediate the problem, (4) specification of treatment goals, and (5) evaluation of progress toward meeting those goals.

Group Therapy

An effective method of dealing with adolescent problems is group therapy. Groups vary according to purpose. Some groups focus on specific problems and limit participation to individuals experiencing such problems (e.g., drug abusers, unwed mothers), whereas others include adolescents experiencing more generalized adjustment difficulties. Some groups are time limited and meet for only a specified number of sessions. Other groups are ongoing, with participants shifting in and out. Some are structured and focus on teaching specific skills (e.g., social skills, assertiveness), and others are open-ended and less structured.

Groups are valuable since they allow for sharing problems and for the camaraderie that results from the knowledge that others experience difficulties similar to one's own. Groups may offer emotional support to the troubled adolescent, aid in developing problem-solving strategies, and provide an environment where the adolescent may practice newly acquired skills.

One technique employed in some groups is role playing. Situations experienced by adolescents are acted out in the therapy room. Adolescents may assume different roles and gain insight into why other individuals react the way they do. Role playing allows the adolescent to practice new behaviors and skills before attempting them outside the group.

Family Therapy

Family therapy is an effective method of dealing with adolescent problems, particularly when the problems involve

126

other family members. Family therapy is similar to group therapy with the exception that the group consists only of family members. The focus of family therapy is on family problems and on reaching mutually agreeable solutions to such problems. It may include a clarification and definition of each family member's roles and responsibilities within the family unit. An attempt is usually made to get family members to discuss problems, establish goals, and gain insight into one another's feelings and behavior. Some goals of family therapy are to improve the stability and functioning of the family, to improve members' relationships, and to enable the family to solve future problems without the assistance of a therapist.

Parent Counseling

There is much that parents can do to alleviate adolescent problems. In some situations, the adolescent will not admit the existence of a problem. Such adolescents may be uncooperative or refuse to participate in treatment. In other instances, problems may be created or worsened through a parent's actions or lack of information and skills on how to handle adjustment problems. Parent counseling can help in such situations.

The focus of parent counseling is typically on instructing parents in adolescent behavior and methods that can be employed to deal with behavior problems. Depending on the problem, parents are aided in gaining insight into their own behavior and how it affects that of the adolescent. Parents might be instructed on how to improve communication with their adolescent and how to manage their offspring better.

Halfway Houses, Group Homes, Therapeutic Communities, and Inpatient Care

In a small number of cases, more intensive treatment is required than can be offered on an outpatient basis. Such situations include instances where the adolescent poses a threat of physical harm to self or others, life-threatening situations (e.g., potential suicide), cases of antisocial and delinquent behavior, some cases of alcohol and drug addiction, or in instances where there is serious family instability.

Inpatient care or placement in halfway houses, group homes, or therapeutic communities is viewed as a treatment of last resort and should only be used when other, less restrictive alternatives have been exhausted.

Inpatient care is typically employed in life-threatening situations and where the adolescent displays symptoms of acute emotional disturbance. Medical and psychiatric care and counseling and psychotherapy are usually offered.

Halfway houses, group homes, and therapeutic communities usually provide long-term treatment and rehabilitation. Adolescents with serious drug and alcohol problems or those who display severe antisocial and delinquent behavior are usually referred to such facilities. The goal is to provide an atmosphere where the adolescent can be rehabilitated to normal functioning and then can return to his or her home community.

In this chapter we have attempted to provide general information about those individuals who provide mental health services for adolescents, the types of services available, and how to obtain help. We have not attempted to discuss every profession, agency, or program involved with adolescents or every treatment procedure. Local resources differ, and many fine programs that exist in only a limited number of communities were omitted. The search for quality services is a difficult one. The purpose of this chapter has been to provide a reference for the initial mental health contact.

part III

PROMOTING
HEALTHY
RELATIONSHIPS

This section offers a guide for promoting constructive and growth-producing relationships. The focus is on family relationships, particularly among adolescents and adults. However, the suggestions and techniques included are helpful in a variety of situations. The art of constructive communication is presented, and a guide for achieving compromises between adults and adolescents is offered.

chapter 10

Constructive Communication

Sarah is a fourteen-year-old eighth grader who was referred to the Counseling Center by the local Youth Court. Her mother complained to the judge that Sarah has been sneaking out with her boyfriend late at night and that several stolen items were recently discovered in her dresser drawer. Sarah is physically attractive and popular at school; she is an honor-roll student. During the first counseling session, Sarah refused to speak while her mother was in the room. Her mother offered an exhaustive list of complaints about Sarah's behavior and personality. All the while, Sarah stared blankly at the floor and refused to respond to her mother's remarks. We learned that Sarah's mother perceived her as "dishonest," "irresponsible," "undisciplined," "selfish," and "arrogant." Anger and hostility predominated her mother's verbal tone and facial expressions. The attack grew so forceful and relentless that Sarah's mother was calmly asked to leave the room for a time. As her mother left the room, tears were streaming down Sarah's face, and she began to speak. She stated that she hated her mother because of all the unkind remarks and accusations. She indicated that she is not allowed privileges that her peers enjoy. Further, she blamed her mother for her father's having left the home last year. Sarah openly admitted that her incorrigible behavior was an attempt to aggravate her mother. Amidst all of the bitter feelings expressed by both parties, there was a hint of mutual respect and concern. Subsequent to clearing the atmosphere of the tremendous tension and anger, both parties agreed to try to reconcile the relationship and change the course of the destructive modes of communication. With the aid of counseling inventories, videotape equipment, intensive communication exercises and behavior compromises in contract form, considerable improvement in the quality of the relationship was observed in the counseling sessions.

The ability to interact with others in a positive and effective manner is an art that requires considerable skill and concentration. Although many people are quite adept at this, others become "bogged down" in negative communication patterns. This may be particularly apparent in the adolescent's relationship with parents and other authority figures. Among young people referred for counseling, communication with adults is too often defensive, hostile, angry, or even nonexistent. Negative labels such as "lazy," "irresponsible," or "selfish" are frequently exchanged. A simple exercise clearly reveals the destructive nature of the communication pattern. Each party is asked to identify positive and negative qualities of the other individual. Provided that the communication process has been disturbed for an extended period of time, a seemingly endless list of criticisms will readily be expressed by each person. When attention is turned toward positive traits, silence prevails!

Unfortunately, ineffective communication is commonplace in daily living. Most people have felt misunderstood, ignored, rejected, or disparaged during a serious attempt to communicate with another person. Given the imprecision of our use of language and the prevalent lack of training in constructive communication, interactions with others are too often dissatisfying. Communication "breakdowns" may create anger, frustration, resentment, hurt, and a variety of other negative emotions. These feelings are magnified in adolescents, who may lack the skills to articulate their emotions. This may lead to withdrawal and further discontent.

Psychologists and counselors have systematically studied communication processes. Several elements necessary for constructive communication have been observed and explained. Skillful and sensitive use of the combined elements of constructive communication creates an atmosphere conducive to meaningful, satisfying interpersonal relationships. Although the principles of constructive communication are generally the same for all ages, the following discussion is tailored to adult–adolescent interactions.

LISTENING

Perhaps the most important skill in effective communication is the ability to *listen*. Listening, a seemingly simple task, is actually a complex behavior that requires intense concentration. Effective listening requires an erect body position while leaning slightly toward the speaker (e.g., the adolescent). One's face should be on the same level with the adolescent's. Sometimes adults literally "talk down" to the shorter adolescent. Other errors in body and facial positioning include slouching in the chair, poor eye contact, sitting too close to or too far from the person (appropriate distance is usually 4 to 5 feet), or sitting in a defensive posture with arms folded across the chest. Your interest and concern are reflected in an erect, upright, and "open" body stance.

Listening is facilitated by a relatively quiet environment that is free of potential interruptions. Depending on the importance of the discussion, you should consider locking the doors, disconnecting the phone, and turning off the radio or television. It is unwise to embark on an in-depth, personal discussion while in the presence of others.

Once a discussion has been initiated, listen intently. It is helpful just to summarize what the young person has said and to point out feelings that he or she experiences in relation to each topic of discussion. This process of simply reflecting the adolescent's concerns through paraphrasing the content of conversation enhances self-exploration and understanding and sets the stage for mature, rational decision making.

RESPECT

In addition to demonstrating effective listening skills, the adult should be able to show *respect* for the adolescent. Respect may be demonstrated in several ways. First, one should allot a minimum amount of time each day solely to communication. During these "talk periods," the adult should delay or withhold critical judgments concerning what the young person has said. Snap judgments and critical remarks usually cause the adolescent to find more sympathetic listeners. If the adult disagrees with the adolescent's point of view, a conversation about values and morality may be pursued in a calm, understanding tone. One of the surest ways to diminish effective communication is to ignore the other's strong need to express individual attitudes and ideas.

EMPATHY

The adult who is communicating effectively must also be able to show *empathy*. Empathy is the ability to perceive and experience the world from the perspective of the other. This is perhaps the most difficult element of communication to master. The problem of demonstrating empathy is compounded by the fact that the adult and the adolescent may be far removed in terms of age, daily experience, and vocabulary. True expressions of empathy serve to facilitate rapport, cohesiveness, and trust. The task of developing empathetic responses requires you to clearly imagine yourself embedded in the same set of circumstances as those confronting the person with whom you are communicating. Then, you must be able to express the experience accurately in terms of feelings and perceptions. Wordiness, difficult vocabulary, and abstraction should be avoided. If your perceptions are inaccurate, the other individual will usually correct you. If this happens, acknowledge the correction so that empathy is achieved and an opportunity to complete the discussion is attained.

GENUINENESS

Emphasis on openness and honesty in relationships has increased throughout the past few years. Psychologists maintain that *genuineness* is an essential component of effective communication. Words such as *openness, honesty, sincerity,* and *transparency* characterize the concept of genuineness. To be genuine in a relationship is to behave in a manner that is truly representative of your innermost thoughts, ideas, feelings, and attitudes. To do this, you must be willing to take the risk of disclosing yourself in a genuine manner. It is often easier to offer a facade or a mask for others to accept or reject. Because most of us want to be accepted by others, we often present false pictures of ourselves. This "phoniness" is readily perceived, particularly by adolescents, and serves to block communication channels. Most of us are able to remember feeling repulsed or embarrassed in response to another's phony statement or behavior. It is also embarrassing to catch yourself in this "act." In conclusion, let down your defenses, speak openly and honestly, and spontaneously express genuine feelings.

CONCRETENESS

As stated, the purpose of creating an atmosphere conducive to positive communication is to increase self-exploration. This, in turn, leads to action in the form of effective decision making or problem solving. Communication must be concrete to bridge the gap between exploration and action. As long as stated concerns are vague, solutions to them will also remain vague, and action will be ineffective. Concreteness is achieved by pinpointing specific feelings associated with specific situations and behaviors. Avoid speaking in vague, abstract terms, particularly when the conversation is focused on a problem area. It is easier to speak in vague generalities when disclosing threatening or otherwise uncomfortable material.

PITFALLS

Omission of any of the basic elements of constructive communication mentioned earlier will result in inadequate communication. Each party should be attentive, respectful, empathetic, genuine, and concrete while participating in a conversation or discussion.

One of the most frequent impediments to the communication process is the use of labels. Labeling a person violates virtually all the elements of positive communication. Additionally, labels convey very little information that is useful in solving problem situations. Most labels create a threatening environment that readily lends itself to defensiveness and continued labeling. The discussion is generally short and destructive, leaving bitter feelings with everyone involved.

Questions often interfere with the effective communication process. Most questions do not stimulate in-depth, satisfying conversations but merely render yes–no responses. Particularly stifling questions begin with *when*, *where*, and *why*. Questions beginning with these words elicit short, factual answers that circumvent the elements required for constructive communication. If a question must be asked, it is more optimal to begin with *what* or *how*. These words tend to elicit more involved responses that provide more extensive material necessary for a satisfying discussion.

Other more obvious pitfalls include *talking too much or too little*. Too much talking frustrates and confuses the listener, particularly when he or she is disclosing deeply personal thoughts. The person may feel that the other party is disinterested or unconcerned. A common reaction is for the person to steer the conversation to less important (thereby safer and less threatening) topics. On the other hand, too little talking may also reflect a lack of interest and may encourage "rambling." An appropriate amount of conversation will structure the discussion and express interest and concern. As a rule of thumb, each party should offer between 40 and 60 percent of the conversation. Speaking more or less than these percentages usually obstructs the verbal exchange.

Too often, communication is *indirect*. This is the common mistake of saying one thing and meaning another. For example, a parent who is requesting that the yard be mowed shouldn't ask if the adolescent is tired. Rather, the request should be stated in a direct manner specifying the intent (e.g., "Please mow the yard before going with your friends.")

It is helpful to employ as many of the elements of constructive communication as possible and to avoid the pitfalls. If a seriously destructive pattern of communication has evolved, a qualified counselor or psychologist should be contacted.

chapter 11

The Art
(and Science)
of Compromise

The ability to resolve conflict among family members is just as important as the ability to communicate constructively. Conflict, as defined here, occurs when the behavior of a family member is at odds with the expectations of another family member. Conflict, in this sense, is inevitable throughout all developmental stages. However, it is amplified in the adolescent period because of rapidly changing social roles, responsibilities, and expectations. All too often, minor conflicts produce resentment, hostility, and a general breakdown in communication. Resentment may turn to retribution that creates the opportunity for spiteful (e.g., passive-aggressive) behavior, leading to further conflict.

This cycle may be prevented in several ways. First, expectations for the behavior of other family members should be stated clearly and specifically. For example, parents who expect their children to be home at certain hours should state the precise time rather than the familiar "Don't be too late." Teenagers should also be specific in citing their expectations of parental behavior. Second, conflict is often avoided by refusing to participate in battles that cannot be won. For example, parents cannot, no matter how hard they try, coerce teenagers into selecting a particular group of friends or attaining a certain grade point average. On the other hand, adolescents are hard pressed to change parental attitudes about dating, sex, money, or drinking. Disputes over these topics are, for the most part, unnecessary and avoidable. Finally, parents should recognize that privileges may be administered as rewards for responsible behavior rather than being given according to an arbitrarily prescribed set of standards that ignores responsible behavior.

The sixteen-year-old who is a good student, helps around the house, holds a part-time job, and obeys the law is obviously more deserving of using the family car than his seventeen-year-old brother who is constantly in trouble at school. Increasing freedom with increasing responsibility is a useful initiative.

RESOLVING CONFLICTS WITH CONTRACTS

Written contracts are effective aids in both the prevention and resolution of conflict. This is a means of (1) clearly stating expectations, (2) avoiding emotionally charged verbal exchanges, and (3) rewarding desirable, responsible behavior. Contracts have long been useful instruments in preventing and resolving conflicts in legal and business spheres, and they are equally applicable to conflicts within the family arena. Contracts nearly always require compromise in the form of clearly stated behaviors expected of all persons entering the contract. Contracts should follow these guidelines:

1. Expectations of participants clearly and specifically outlined.
2. Time limits for behaviors.
3. Penalties or consequences of noncompliance.
4. Signatures of all participants.

An example of a contract follows. Such contracts can be extremely flexible. As these compromises are achieved, new behaviors or expectations may be added as old ones are phased out. Agreements like this one are readily achieved, provided that each party shows a willingness to study the perspectives of other family members and to grant concessions for compromises offered by others. Some degree of flexibility is required for all compatible and satisfying relationships.

CONTRACT

Date _____

Bill agrees to:

1. Mow yard weekly

2. Use phone only fifteen minutes daily

3. Be home by 10:00 P.M.

4. Discontinue use of family car for one week if contract is broken

Mom and Dad agree to:

1. Pay Bill $5 each Friday afternoon

2. Discontinue all discussion about style or length of Bill's hair

3. Pay Bill $25 if contract is broken

Bill	*Mom*	*Dad*
Bill	Mom	Dad

Another form of a contract is the token economy. This system is based on the idea that tokens or points are awarded for desirable behaviors and can be exchanged for rewards and privileges. A token economy is preferred when several behaviors are expected on a routine basis. This system enables the participants to observe and record a number of activities systematically and to administer rewards for responsible behavior. An example of a token economy follows.

TOKEN ECONOMY							
Responsibilities	M	T	W	T	F	S	S
1. Clean room	1		1	1	1	1	1
2. Study one hour	1	1	1	1	1	1	1
3. Speak 15 minutes with brother			1	1		1	1
4. Empty garage		1	1	1	1		1
5. Home by 10:00 P.M.		1	1	1	1	1	1
Privileges							
1. Use car	2	2		2			2
2. $5 allowance					5		
3. Movie on weekend						5	
4. Trip to the coast							
Cumulative Total	0	2	7	8	8	7	10

Bill	*Mom*	*Dad*
Bill	Mom	Dad

The Art (and Science) of Compromise

Effective token economies have clearly stated expectations (responsibilities) and rewards (privileges). Points are assigned for successful completion of these tasks and are used to obtain the privileges. Point values for privileges should be fixed in such a way that daily and weekly privileges can be obtained with remaining points that can be applied to long-range goals such as a "trip to the coast." A cumulative total is recorded at the bottom of the chart by adding the number of points remaining from the day before to the number of points left over that day. For example, on Tuesday, Bill earned four points and used two for the family car, leaving two for the day. Those two points were added to no (zero) remaining points from the day before, yielding a cumulative score of two.

It is important to remember several guidelines when implementing this program. First, remaining points cannot be applied to the next week's privileges. All remaining points should be applied to one long-range project that does not occur on a weekly basis. Motivation quickly diminishes when saved points can be exchanged for daily and weekly privileges. Bill must earn the five points he exchanges for the $5 allowance during the week that the allowance is awarded. Second, parents should not discontinue the program if the adolescent states that he or she will not participate. We have found that most adolescents will comply with the program (1) if allowed some participation in its design and (2) if convinced that their parents seriously intend to implement the program over a given period of time. Finally, it is essential that all participants be consistent in their approach to the program. Changes in the token economy must be supported by all participants. No loans or advances of points are allowed, and no exceptions are permitted. These kinds of exchanges will rapidly decrease the motivational power of the program.

Contracts and token economies are useful tools in creating satisfactory compromises. Resolving conflicts objectively, in an atmosphere free of negative feelings, can pave the way for more fruitful and satisfying family relations. Contracts and token economies are designed to be short-term procedures for intervention whenever conflict arises. We do not advocate their continual use throughout adolescence.

part IV

THE
TRANSITIONAL
PERIOD

There are a variety of tasks that must be achieved before the older adolescent is considered an autonomously functioning adult. Several of these tasks are mentioned, and two are discussed in detail. We consider mate selection and career development to be extremely vital tasks that most adolescents encounter during this period. Unfortunately, many adolescents are inadequately prepared to satisfy their needs in these areas. Methods of preparation and topics of consideration concerning mate selection and career development are offered in this section.

chapter *12*

Late Adolescence

The process of establishing oneself as an independent, autonomous adult is marked by a period of transition. Such important matters as financial independence, career development, and mate selection typically confront the maturing adolescent. Both parents and adolescents generally strive for the adolescent's independence; yet there is often difficulty in severing the mutual, sometimes stifling dependence that characterizes many parent–child relationships. All the while, the maturing adolescent is confronted with other important developmental tasks. The following discussion focuses on two critical aspects of this transitional period: mate selection and career development.

MATE SELECTION

With divorce rates rising, it is worthwhile to examine the critical elements involved in choosing a mate or marital partner. Late adolescence or early adulthood is the usual time of marriage in our society. There are a number of forces that encourage marriage at this age, including (1) a need for personal and sexual intimacy, (2) moral constraints on sexual behavior outside of marriage, (3) the tendency to displace dependency on one's parents with a more mature, heterosexual relationship, and (4) economic independence. Forces that encourage commitment to enduring relationships vary with individuals, and there is considerable pressure to engage in such relationships. Hence, it is important for couples to analyze their relationship in exquisite, systematic detail, covering a number of critical topics prior to making a serious emotional and legal commitment. Although this approach may seem callous, objective evaluation of each individual's background, habits, attitudes, and interests may prevent future conflict.

It is essential to examine the family composition and background of the other person. One should look at such variables as age, occupation, educational level, and religious affiliation of family members. These may serve as predictors of certain aspects of the future relationship. It is helpful to examine closely the nature of the relationship between the individual and his or her family. Frequently, a spouse discovers that he or she takes a back seat to in-laws, which can result in jealousy or resentment.

In-depth discussion concerning career and occupational plans is helpful in avoiding conflict. Many people simply assume that their spouses will or will not join the work force without the benefit of explicitly stated intentions. Today's financially demanding society often dictates that both partners be wage earners, yet some husbands feel threatened by the idea of a wife working outside the home. On the other hand, husbands may come to resent bitterly their unemployed spouses. The reverse is often true as well. The type of work, anticipated amount of time to be spent in the job setting, and expected income should be explored.

Money is the source of serious conflict in a vast number of relationships. Too often, there are misunderstandings about the use of money after a formal commitment to the relationship has been made. Each partner should discuss personal philosophies and attitudes concerning family money management. One approach involves pooling the family income, deducting household expenses, and making joint decisions about residual money. Other couples have opted to share equally in the household expenses while each partner retains his or her respective income for personal use. There are as many approaches to money management as there are families; however, it is helpful to clarify attitudes as early as possible.

Children are often the source of considerable tension in family relationships. In modern society, a decision not to have children is acceptable and certainly feasible, given contemporary methods of birth control. People differ with respect to how many children they desire as well as specifically when they plan pregnancy. Most importantly, individuals vary in their attitudes about discipline and behavior management. Most parents tend to discipline their children as their parents disciplined them. Lack of education in this area in addition to the absence of generally accepted methods of child management create confusion and conflict. Child-rearing discussions are prone to be emotionally laden because of their associations with religious doctrine and family tradition. For these reasons, general philosophies and attitudes concerning the family structure should be discussed prior to the inception of a family.

Religious orientation and expectations about family spiritual life should be given serious attention. For many individuals, religious life is the most important aspect of existence. Family spiritual nourishment is derived through shared beliefs and common participation in religious rituals. The nature and degree of commitment to religious doctrine vary greatly among families and individuals. It is certainly advisable for young couples to discuss religious ideas and to state explicitly the expectations they have of their partners. Examples of expectations include moral codes, methods of religious practice, financial commitment to religious organizations, and religious affiliation of children.

Sexual incompatibility is another difficulty that can often be avoided through planning and discussion. Couples should consider such variables as frequency and variety in sexual expression. One spouse may desire sexual contact daily, whereas the other is more comfortable with weekly experiences. Moreover, there is considerable variety in the types of sexual expression that are satisfying to couples. An act that is thoroughly satisfying and enticing to one individual may be repulsive to the other. These potential differences should not be ignored!

Another volatile area is the allocation of responsibility for household maintenance. Typical traditional roles in which the male washes the car and empties the garbage while the female cooks, cleans, sews, shops, cares for the children, and essentially maintains the home have disintegrated during the past few years. The increasing number of women in the labor force makes it impractical for the woman to assume the vast majority of responsibility in the home. In most instances, a more equal distribution of household chores is mandated. Again, attitudes and behavior vary; yet it is advisable to settle differences in this area as soon as possible.

The preceding is by no means an exhaustive list of areas of potential marital conflict. These and other areas are best explored with a minister, marriage counselor, family doctor, or mental health professional.

VOCATIONAL CHOICE

What do you want to be when you grow up? This question, answered frivolously and naively by children, takes on particular importance during adolescence. Vocational choice may be viewed as a narrowing process, with reality and economic necessity replacing the naiveté and impracticality of youth. For the child, vocations offering glamour and excitement are most attractive (e.g., movie star, celebrity, athlete, cowboy, astronaut). As the person matures, many other factors, admittedly more mundane, take precedence.

The transition from adolescence to adulthood is

marked, in part, by the achievement of economic independence and entrance into the world of work (or selection of and active training for a particular vocation). Vocational choice becomes increasingly important as the individual reaches late adolescence and comes face to face with the impending necessity of earning an independent living.

Vocational choice is determined by cumulative selective factors that operate from childhood to narrow one's choices increasingly. These factors, which interact in complex ways, include intelligence, special abilities, interests, personality, parental influences, socioeconomic factors, educational experiences, and vocational information.

Intelligence, special abilities, interests, and personality narrow the field of possible vocational choices. Each vocation has its own set of specific characteristics that the individual must possess to be successful. Think for a moment of the personal attributes of a skilled surgeon, teacher, artisan, psychologist, musician, athlete, or businessperson. Personality factors such as motivation, persistence, degree of extroversion or introversion, frustration tolerance, ability to postpone gratification (necessary for individuals entering professions that require long periods of schooling), ability to withstand stress, and willingness to take risks may determine the type of career one chooses.

Sex has traditionally been a factor that limited vocational choice. Increasingly, however, it is becoming irrelevant as sex-role stereotypes fall to the assault of diverse human potential. We now have growing numbers of men who are nurses, telephone operators, and child-care specialists; and more and more women are becoming lawyers, engineers, even dock workers.

Parental and socioeconomic influences steer the adolescent toward certain vocations and away from others. Parental expectations of their children, as well as their evaluation of the acceptability of certain vocations, will influence the adolescent's career choice. Upper-class parents generally value occupations that require extended formal education and advanced academic training (e.g., law, medicine, business). Blue-collar occupations are typically viewed as unacceptable. Lower-class parents, though they may hold high expectations for their children, may find it economically impossible to finance their adolescent's education. Economic necessity may require entrance to a vocation requiring less formal training.

Educational experiences and access to vocational information are quite important in career choice. The scope and quality of the adolescent's high-school curriculum, the variety of courses offered, and the stress placed on career education will influence vocational choice. Many high schools offer both academic (precollege) and vocational–technical programs. Vocational–technical programs provide training in a particular trade and prepare the adolescent for entrance to the job market following graduation.

Regardless of the particular marital and vocational avenues selected by the adolescent, careful planning and informed decisions are helpful tools in making a smooth transition into effective adult living.

References and Suggested Readings

American Psychiatric Association. *Diagnostic and Statistical Manual of Mental Disorders* (2nd ed.). Washington, D.C.: American Psychiatric Association, 1968.

AUSUBELL, D. P. *Theory and Problems of Adolescent Development.* New York: Grune & Stratton, 1954.

BANDURA, A. The Stormy Decade: Fact or Fiction? *Psychology in the Schools,* 1964, I, 224–231.

BRECKER, E. M. *Licit and Illicit Drugs.* Mount Vernon, N.Y.: Consumers Union, 1972.

BREHM, S. S. *Help for Your Child: A Parent's Guide to Mental Health Services.* Englewood Cliffs, N.J.: Prentice-Hall, 1978.

DE ROPP, ROBERT S. *Drugs and the Mind.* New York: St. Martin's Press, 1957, pp. 157–158.

DWYER, J., & MAYER, J. Psychological Effects of Variations in Physical Appearance During Adolescence. *Adolescence,* 1968–69, *3,* 353–368.

ERIKSON, E. H. Identity and the Life Cycle. *Psychological Issues* (Vol. I, No. 1). New York: International Universities Press, 1959.

FEINSTEIN, SHERMAN C., & GIOVACCHINI, PETER L. *Adolescent Psychiatry.* Chicago: University of Chicago Press, 1978.

FREEDMAN, A. M., KAPLAN, H. I., & SADOCK, B. J., eds. *Comprehensive Textbook of Psychiatry (2nd ed.) (2 vols.).* Baltimore: Williams & Wilkins, 1975.

GRINDLER, ROBERT E. *Adolescence.* New York: John Wiley, 1973.

HORROCKS, J. E. *The Psychology of Adolescence.* Boston: Houghton Mifflin, 1976.

HURLOCK, E. B. *Adolescent Development.* New York: McGraw-Hill, 1973.

KATCHADOURIAM, H. *The Biology of Adolescence.* San Francisco: W. H. Freeman & Company Publishers, 1977.

McCANDLESS, B. R. *Adolescents: Behavior and Development.* Hinsdale, Ill.: Dryden Press, 1970.

MEYER, WILLIAM J. *Readings in the Psychology of Childhood and Adolescence.* Waltham, Mass.: Blaisdell Publishing Company, 1967.

MUUSS, R. E., ed. *Adolescent Behavior and Society: A Book of Readings.* New York: Random House, 1975.

MUUSS, R. E. *Theories of Adolescence.* New York: Random House, 1975.

PARK, C. C., & SHAPIRO, L. N. *You Are Not Alone.* Boston: Atlantic-Little, Brown, 1976.

POWELL, M. *The Psychology of Adolescence (2nd ed.). Indianapolis: Bobbs-Merrill, 1971.*

QUAY, HERBERT C., & WERRY, JOHN S. *Psychopathological Disorders of Childhood.* New York: John Wiley, 1979.

SCHENK, Q. F., & SCHENK, E. L. *Pulling Up Roots.* Englewood Cliffs, N.J.: Prentice-Hall, 1978.

TWIFORD, RAINER. *A Child With a Problem: A Guide to the Psychological Disorders of Children.* Englewood Cliffs, N.J.: Prentice-Hall, 1979.

WALEM, S., HAUSERMAM, N. M., & LAVIN, P. J. *Clinical Guide to Behavior Therapy.* Baltimore: Williams & Wilkins, 1977.

WEINSWIG, M. H. *Use and Misuse of Drugs Subject to Abuse.* New York: Pegasus, 1975.

Index

Acne, 15
Adjustment, 6–11, 34–36, 96–101
Adolescence:
  as adjustment period, 6–11; conflict in (see Conflict); defined, 4–5; mate selection, 155–58; personality development (see Personality development); as phenomenon of industrial age, 5–6; preadolescent development and, 11–12; pubescence and puberty, 12–16; relationships (see Communication, constructive; Compromise); vocational choice, 158–60
Adrenal cortex, 12
Aggressive reaction of adolescence, 101–5
Alcohol, 57–63
"Alternative" theory of drug use, 57
Androgens, 12
Anorexia nervosa, 111–14
Anterior pituitary glands, 12

Bandura, Albert, 27–28
Barbiturates, 63–64
Behavior disorder, 101–5
Body growth, 11–12

Children, marital conflict and, 156–57
Children's service programs, 123
Clergy, as source of help, 119
Cocaine, 59, 69–70
Codeine, 65
College counseling centers, 123
Collins, John Peyton, 80
Communication, constructive, 134–42
  concreteness, 140; empathy, 138–39; genuineness, 139–40; listening, 137–38; pitfalls, 141–42; respect, 138
Community mental health centers, 121–23
Community resources, 121–24
Compromise, 144–49
Concreteness, 140

164

Conflict:
Marital, 156–58; resolution of, 144–49
Contracts, 145–49
Corticotropic hormones, 12
Counseling, 123–25, 127
Crisis lines, 124

Delinquency (see Unlawful behavior)
Delirium tremens (D.T.'s), 62
Depressants, 56–57, 60–67
Drug use and abuse, 56–75
alcohol, 57–63; causes, 58–60; depressants, 56–57, 60–67; guidance 74–75; hallucinogens, 56, 57, 71–74 marijuana, 56, 57, 59, 71–72 stimulants, 68–70
Durkheim, Emile, 90

Empathy, 138–39
Environmental deteriminants of behavior, 24–25
Erikson, Erik, 24, 33
Estrogens, 12

Family service programs, 123
Family therapy, 126–27
Freud, Anna, 26–27

Genuineness, 139–40
Gesell, Arnold, 24
Gonadotropic hormones, 12
Gonads, 12
Group homes, 128
Group therapy, 126
Guidance counselors, 118

Hair growth, 14, 15
Halfway houses, 128
Hall, G. Stanley, 24, 26
Hallucinogens, 56, 57, 71–74
Heightened emotionality, 7
Helping professions, 117–21
Heroin, 65
Heterosexual experience, 50–53
Homosexual experience, 49–50

Hormones, 12
Household maintenance, 158
Hysterical neurosis, 105–8

Identity, 33–34
Information services, 124
Inpatient care, 128

Jacob, Jerry, 90–91

Kohlberg, Lawrence, 24

Late adolescence, 153–60
Librium, 64–65
Listening, 137–38
LSD, 56, 57, 72–74

Marijuana, 56, 57, 59, 71–72
Masturbation, 48–49
Mate selection, 155–58
Mead, Margaret, 5–6
Menstruation, 13–14
Methadone, 67
Mothaqualonc, 64
Money, marital conflict and, 156
Morphine, 65

Narcotics, 65–67
Nicotine, 58–59, 68–69
Nocturnal emissions, 42

Opium, 65–66

Parent counseling, 127
Peer groups, 7, 35, 58
Personality development, 17–36
adjustment, 34–36; case histories, 18–21; personality, defined, 21–22; preadolescent, 22–23; self-concept and identity, 30–34; theories of, 23–28; timing of sexual maturity and, 29–30
Personality traits, 21–22
Peyote, 71, 74
Physical changes, 10–16
Physicians, as source of help, 118–19

165